Robert Faricy, S.J.

The Lord's Dealing

The Primacy of the Feminine in Christian Spirituality

Paulist Press
New York and New Jersey

Cover art: "Our Lady of Tenderness," original icon by John Matusiak. Photo by Gene Plaisted. Cover design by Moe Berman.

Library of Congress Cataloging-in-Publication Data

Faricy, Robert L., 1926-
    The Lord's dealing: the primacy of the feminine in Christian
spirituality / Robert Faricy.
    p. cm.
    Includes bibliographies.
    ISBN 0-8091-3003-3 (pbk.) : $6.95 (est.)
    1. Woman (Christian theology) 2. Femininity of God.
  3. Spirituality. 4. Human ecology—Religious aspects—Christianity.
  5. Teilhard de Chardin, Pierre. 6. Jung, C. G. (Carl Gustav),
    1875-1961. I. Title.
    BT704.F37 1988   88-17887
    231—dc19   CIP

Published by Paulist Press
997 Macarthur Boulevard
Mahwah, New Jersey 07430

Printed and bound in the
United States of America

Contents

One
The Suppression of the Feminine   1

Two
Ecology, Woman, Person   6

Three
Jesus and the World   34

Four
God and the Feminine   61

Five
The Body of Christ   77

Six
Conclusions: Ten Theses   98

Appendix
God's Gender and Creation as Feminine   102

Index   106

iii

for Sister Lucy Rooney, S.N.D.

Acknowledgments

This book includes material previously published in *The Teilhard Review* and in the proceedings of the College Theology Society for 1986, volume 32. I want to thank all who have helped me in writing the following chapters, either through recommending books and articles for me to read, through discussion and correspondence, or by reading and suggesting revisions, especially: Francis A. Sullivan, S.J., John Navone, S.J., Jane Mathison, Sister Jane Russell, and Lady Bronwen Astor. And I want to thank those who helped me to prepare the manuscript: Leslie Wearne and Susan Fuller.

The book is written from a Roman Catholic faith perspective, and so accepts the ordinary teaching of the Catholic Church as a theological parameter and guide. It is published with full approval of religious superiors.

Furthermore, I write out of my own background in the Catholic Church in the United States, and in the awareness of the primacy of the feminine intrinsic to my faith, and also of the suppression of the feminine in my Church in my country from the nineteenth century masculinization of Catholicism in favor of Irish male immigrants to the present-day masculinization of the Church in favor of various ideological options.

Writing this book has helped me to understand better my relationship with the Lord, and with others, in the world. I pray that it give you light on the issues it discusses, and that it help you, too, to grow in the understanding of yourself in relation to God, to others, and to the world.

Robert Faricy, S.J.
Pontifical Gregorian University
Rome, Italy
March 25, 1988

" . . . the angel cried: Carpenter, haven't you noticed this is the Lord's dealing?"

Rainer Maria Rilke, "Joseph's Suspicion," in *The Life of the Virgin Mary*, tr. Stephen Spender

1
The Suppression of the Feminine

Adam complained to God about Eve. Mary's pregnancy upset Joseph. No secret: that in the normal order of things in our man's world, women frequently and in many sectors find themselves misunderstood, unjustly treated, even oppressed. And in Western culture at least, the feminine principle has been seriously suppressed correlatively with the psychological and socio-politico-economic oppression of women. Of course these two—the oppression of women and suppression of feminine values and of the feminine principle—inevitably go together.

This book takes up the suppression of the feminine and, especially, the primacy of the feminine in Christian spirituality. In practice, the feminine does not at all hold the primacy, either in Western culture or in the religious culture of Christian churches. Nevertheless, the primacy of the feminine is intrinsic to the Christian good news, even though not always found as a practical reality.

Only to the extent that the feminine is restored to its primacy in Christianity will Christianity find itself in good health. And only to the point that the suppression of the feminine is corrected will our Western culture recover from its many illnesses.

1

What do I mean by "the feminine"? "The feminine" refers to a general (and, to a large extent, impossible to put into
words) principle rooted in feminine experience. The feminine
finds its roots mainly in the experience of woman, but more
generally in the whole "female" side of human experience. We
need to oversimplify here because we are dealing in the largely
inarticulable.

Marilyn French has said it as well as anyone:

> "Masculine" experience is rooted in power-in-the-world,
> with its epitomizing act: to kill. "Feminine" experience is
> rooted in nature with its epitomizing act: to give birth. . . .
> Love is feminine. . . . Life is the highest value for "fem-
> inine" people; whereas control is the highest value for
> "masculine" people.[1]

Christianity is a religion of life, of new life, and a religion
that puts love in first place. So the suppression of the feminine
throws Christianity seriously out of kilter.

To propose the feminine as a universal principle can lead
to trouble and to error. The stereotypes of female passivity and
male aggressivity could encourage us to see feminine and masculine as basically the result of female unwillingness and male
force.[2] This would bring us, almost, to rape as a cultural par-
adigm!

By "the feminine" I do not intend to posit any philosophical universal principle. Here, "the feminine" is a descriptive
term, impossible to fully define, that covers a wide range of
human qualities and values that are better understood intui-
tively than defined and put into order rationally.

The matter is complicated by the fact that, because Western culture is so dominantly masculine, "the feminine" is, to a
great extent, a male construct, a projection of the feminine side
of men.[3] Certainly, "the feminine" is not the reality of women,

not female humanity. In terms of Jungian psychology, our culture has suppressed, even repressed, its "anima," its feminine side. However, the Jungian "anima" itself is a man's idea of the feminine.

What can be done? Here, in this book, I try to use the idea of the feminine without confusing it with the reality of women and without understanding it as an appendage to the masculine, an aspect of the male, a solution for men's problems. The idea of the feminine does have a content that both men and women can grasp. I try to use it accordingly.

The suppression of the feminine has historically involved much more than the oppression of women, although the two are inseparable. In speaking of the suppression of the feminine, we have to consider also the oppression of nature (the ecological problem) and the devaluation of the feminine aspects of culture and of human nature as we find it in both women and men.

The contents of the following chapters pull together certain themes not always considered in their interrelationships: woman and the feminine, the world-as-nature and ecology, the mutuality between God and the world in Jesus Christ risen, and both the church and the world as the body of Christ. In contemporary Western culture, these subjects call for reflection in terms of their relationships with one another.[4] And if we do not take them all together, we will not understand them as well as we might.

The general theological framework for such a reflection needs to include the principal categories of our culture, and especially: evolutionary process, interpersonal relations, and the interdependence of spirit and matter. The chapters that follow rely partly on Carl Jung's psychology, and partly on the historical analysis of some modern writers. But the theological framework is that of Pierre Teilhard de Chardin (1881–1955), the French priest-scientist who has had such an important influence on Christian thought, from liberation theology to contemplative spirituality, and from Vatican II's *Pastoral Constitution on the Church in the Modern World* to the encyclicals of Pope John Paul II.

The suppression of the feminine in Western culture manifests itself in several unfortunate ways. Because of the close association in human consciousness between nature and woman, the relative depersonalization of women and the exploitation of nature have reinforced one another. The devaluation and exploitation of nature can be seen as the suppression of nature-understood-as-feminine.

The suppression of the feminine—in nature, in woman, and generally in culture—can be viewed in terms of a cultural split between nature (as feminine) and person. When nature is devalued for exploitation, so is woman, and so are, inevitably, the feminine aspects of culture. These matters form the subject of the next chapter, which takes as its starting point the ecological crisis arising from human misuse, mismanagement, and blind exploitation of the environment. It finds some of the roots of the suppression of the feminine (in the blind exploitation of nature, the oppression of women, and the devaluation of feminine aspects of culture) in the sixteenth and seventeenth century upheavals in Western culture.[5] And it talks about the suppression of the feminine in contemporary culture and Christianity.

Notes

1. Marilyn French, *Beyond Power: On Women, Men, and Morals* (New York: Summit, 1985), pp. 91–93.

2. As Anne Dickason has shown in "The Feminine as a Universal," *Feminism and Philosophy*, ed. M. Vetterling-Braggin, F. Elliston, and J. English (Totowa, N.J.: Littlefield, Adams, and Co., 1977), pp. 79–100, and especially pp. 97–98.

3. See Rosemary Radford Ruether, *Sexism and God-Talk: Toward a Feminist Theology* (Boston: Beacon Press, 1983), pp. 190–191.

4. I use the word "culture" in its anthropological sense, to refer to language, customs, institutions, technologies, and values characteristic of a given population, or, as the *Encyclopedia Britannica* says, to include "all the learned and standardized forms of behavior" used and expected to be used.

5. Clearly, the suppression of the feminine well pre-dates the sixteenth century. Gerda Lerner traces the origins of oppressive patriarchy to very early times in *The Creation of Patriarchy* (New York: Oxford University Press, 1986). In the history of ideas, the devaluation of the feminine goes back at least to Aristotle; see Joyce A. Little, "Sexual Equality in the Church," *Heythrop Journal*, 27 (1987), p. 166.

2
Ecology, Woman, Person

The modern continuing ecological crisis has many and complex causes. We can identify behind the ecological crisis a broader and deeper problem: the alienation between person and nature in the contemporary Western worldview. This split includes a perceived division and even opposition between:

1. the person and the natural world;
2. man and woman understood as "nature";
3. the person and human nature itself.

These three alienations have in common that they split nature off from person. We can expect, then, to find issues in these three related and mutually influential areas:

1. the ecological crisis: *man against nature;*
2. women's issues: *man against woman;*
3. human life issues (abortion, euthanasia, torture, and all violent oppression of human life as such): *man against himself.*[1]

All three alienations are related. For example, man-against-the-natural-world finds himself, finally, against-hu-

man-nature. Exploitation becomes air and water and soil pollution. Overuse of land turns it into uninhabitable wasteland.
Again, not only does man-against-himself produce a history of
male domination and oppression of women and a reinforce-
ment of patriarchal social structures, but, also, he finds himself
denying the feminine in himself. Alienated from his own human nature, he faces not only a feminist backlash that escalates
his war with woman, but an acerbated consequent war with
himself. And man-exploiting-human-nature by going against
innocent human life reinforces his exploitation of nature and of
women.

This chapter has as its purpose to take a panoramic view
of the above three sets of important problems of our times—
ecological, women's, human life—to see how all three involve
an alienation between person and nature, and to understand
them, therefore, in their fundamental bases and in their relat-
edness to one another. This wide-lens look at ecology, women,
and human life all together necessarily calls for a synthesis in
the shape of a big picture, a hypothesis based on the research,
conclusions, and hypotheses of others, some of whom I refer
to in footnotes.

After sketching this large and panoramic design as an
overall question for ourselves and our times, I try in the last
part of the chapter to show how the thought of Pierre Teilhard
de Chardin provides us with elements of an answer. Teilhard
especially can help us to overcome our split vision of person
and nature by giving us a unified vision where human beings
and the natural world can stand as one in harmony, where the
war between men and women can become a peaceful revolution, where human life finds its true meaning and therefore its
true value, and where all things come together in love in the
unity of one loving Lord, Jesus Christ.

The far-reaching and cross-cutting alienation between
person and nature has many of its historical roots in the Prot-

estant reformation of the sixteenth century and in the scientific revolution of the seventeenth century. Let us take these one at a time, not so much as history as, rather, structural determinants of today's worldview in Western civilization.

Man-Against-Nature: Reformation Protestantism

An article published in 1967 by Lynn White, "The Historical Roots of Our Ecological Crisis," in the periodical *Science*,[2] gave rise to a debate that lasted all through the 1970's and into the 1980's. White argued that "our science and technology have grown out of Christian attitudes toward man's relation to nature which are almost universally held not only by Christians and neo-Christians but also by . . . post-Christians."[3] What are these Christian attitudes so commonly held?

> We are superior to nature, contemptuous of it, willing to use it for our slightest whim. . . . Our present science and our present technology are so tinctured with orthodox Christian arrogance toward nature that no solution for our ecological crisis can be expected from them alone. Since the roots of our trouble are so largely religious, the remedy must also be essentially religious.[4]

Several other authors after White have set out the same thesis with various emphases and from different viewpoints. The basic proposition is that man's contemporary anthropocentric and aggressively exploitative attitude toward nature has its origin in the Judaeo-Christian teaching of human sovereignty over all other creatures, and that this teaching has resulted in a values-blind science and technology and in an insanely consumeristic culture.[5] Christianity stands accused of preaching man's "absolute right of sovereignty over nature."[6] Garrett Hardin has attacked the very idea of a caring God as at the root of bad Western ecological attitudes and practices. He understands the Christian concept of God to have so functioned historically as to deplete human will and initiative to prepare for the future. For Hardin, the enemy of responsible stewardship of nature is not a wrong or incomplete idea of Christian stewardship, but God understood as our Father. "It is high time," he writes, "that we try to reshape human beings into mature creatures who no longer depend on the support of a benevolent Providence under any name."[7]

The charge against Christianity is this: Christian tradition concerning man's relation to nature has depersonalized nature and contributed strongly to a lack of respect for nature. In particular, the creation story of the first chapter of the Book of Genesis demythologizes and depersonalizes nature. And, furthermore, it mandates man to "have dominion" over all of nature, and to "subdue it."[8]

The debate, then, is not about the morality of ruthlessly exploiting nature, but about where the underlying present perception of the person-nature relationship comes from. The debate concerns the origin of the conceptual basis for our exploitative activity.

Several Protestant theologians have defended Christianity against this accusation.[9] They have pointed out that the Christian tradition about the relationship between man and the rest of the natural world leads not to exploitation but rather to stewardship of the earth. Christianity, they submit, teaches us to develop natural resources responsibly and to judiciously administer the natural world as a garden God has given us to tend.

And yet, not all Protestant theologians reject the charges. Lutheran Carl Braaten, for example, writes that "it is difficult to gainsay the Christian responsibility for the rape of nature,"[10] and goes so far as to condemn the eschatological theologies of Rudolph Bultmann, Friedrich Gogarten, and Gerhard Ebeling as de-naturing the future. They have made the Gospel "good news to men but bad news for the world" because their theologies promote the old and still much alive exploitative approach to the natural world.[11]

It seems to me that at the origin of the contemporary aggressively exploitative attitude toward the world of nature lies as a partial cause not Christianity as such, but the Christianity of the Protestant reformation. And many Protestant theologians, Americans in particular, mean—when they say "Christianity"—a general reformation kind of Protestant Christianity.

One idea of the Protestant reformation has special importance: the Lutheran idea that all nature has fallen and lies under God's judgment; and human nature, then, is essentially sinful. This is not to deny that Martin Luther (1483–1546) "had a deep appreciation for nature and for the presence of God in nature."[12] But when in the evolution of Western civilization these pessimistic and negative ideas about nature cut loose from Christian faith and floated freely into the mainstream of our culture, they pervaded our attitude toward nature with pragmatism and utilitarianism toward nature.

An important influence has been that of Luther's idea of the two kingdoms.[13] In the Lutheran perspective, and in the general perspective of much Protestant theology, the kingdom of Christ and the kingdom of the world are understood as in tension, in antithesis, in some kind of opposition. The same opposition holds between God's rule of power in the world and his rule of grace through the Gospel, between the church and the world, and between the order of creation and the order of salvation. The Christian, then, finds himself in antithetical opposition to nature. The Protestant tradition has read God's mandate to man, in Genesis, chapter one, that man exercise dominion over nature and subdue it, in the framework of this two-kingdom theology. Result: an approach to nature that understands man as against nature. His stewardship stands within a master-slave relationship where man is the master over nature as slave or servant of man.

Reformation Protestantism, in its conceptions of the two kingdoms and of fallen human nature, has separated the order of creation from the order of redemption. The order of creation, including all of nature, stands—corrupt and sinful—under God's wrath. This negative view of nature calls for aggressivity on man's part to make nature a good slave.

Helmut Thielicke serves as a good example of a contemporary Lutheran theologian on the person-nature relationship. Operating out of a Lutheran conception of nature, Thielicke parallels Genesis 9:1-2 ("And God blessed Noah and his sons, and said to them, 'Be fruitful and multiply, and fill the earth. The fear of you and the dread of you shall be upon every beast of the earth, and upon every bird of the air, upon everything that creeps on the ground and on all the fish of the sea; into your hand they are delivered' ") and Genesis 1:28 ("And God said to them, 'Be fruitful and multiply, and fill the earth and subdue it; and have dominion over the fish of the sea and over the birds of the air and over every living thing that moves upon the earth' "). The differences in the two parallel texts indicate the radical change in nature after the fall. Fear, dread and terror hold a fallen and rebellious creation in check. Our dominion over nature now, after the fall, is one of power-to-be-exercised to inculcate terror and dread in nature. Our relationship with nature is not one of harmonious complementarity, but a relationship of master to unruly servant or slave.[14]

Man-Against-Nature: Modern Science

On the heels of the beginnings of the Protestant reformation came that other great determinant of modern culture, especially in the historically Protestant and technologically more advanced countries: the scientific revolution. The new science in the seventeenth century, as today, saw man as against nature.

Many have called Francis Bacon (1561–1626) the father of modern science. Certainly and at least, his ideas had a major influence on the cultural attitudes that came to underlie modern scientific culture. And, as an historical figure, he represents in a naive and quite clear mode the fundamental characteristics of the scientific spirit. Bacon, in his writings, "transformed tendencies already extant in his own society into a total program advocating the control of nature for human benefit." He "fashioned a new ethic sanctioning the exploitation of nature."[15]

Bacon saw nature as unruly disorder, calling out to be tamed, dominated, ordered, and put to work. He transformed the medieval tradition of alchemy by stressing the need to dominate nature not just for the alchemist or magician, but for all of mankind. No longer the alchemist, servant of nature, but the scientist, nature's master. And nature passes from the position of teacher to the role of man's slave.

Our contemporary mechanical view of nature dates back to Bacon's time. The seventeenth century moved beyond the earlier understanding of nature as an organic totality with a kind of soul of its own and mysteries to teach, to the new view of nature as mechanical, as an object to be explored and exploited, mined, channeled, ordered, made man's slave and submissive yielder of secrets, fruits, and profits for man. "I am come in very truth," he writes in *The Masculine Birth of Time*, "leading you Nature with all her children to bind her to your service and make her your slave."[16]

Jane Mathison, in her paper given at the 1984 Teilhard Conference, quoted Albert Schweitzer when he identified Francis Bacon as "the man who drafted the program of the modern world view." And she added that

Bacon was a child of his time, active in rejecting the Aristotelian-medieval-scholastic world view, and working to replace it with . . . "the New Philosophy." Like his contemporaries Galileo and Descartes he insisted that *true* knowledge could be obtained only by reason and experiment.[17]

Bacon's contemporary, Galileo Galilei (1564–1642) met overwhelming opposition from the Vatican because he stood for the mechanistic view of the universe. In Galileo's view, the bible and the church "were essentially about achieving salvation, and as such had no authority to comment on the New Philosophy whose task was the discovery of the 'immutable laws of nature' through the use of reason and experiment."[18] Science and religion have equal status, but quite distinct realms. "Thus Galileo cleaved the world of experimental knowledge from the domain of values."[19] Instinctively, Galileo's ecclesiastical opponents understood that Galileo and the new science wanted to divorce values from nature. And they insisted, vainly, with the same kind of resistance to the devalorizing of nature that we find so often in history on the part of the Catholic Church, from Galileo to *Humanae vitae*.

René Descartes (1596–1650) contributed to the modern scientific worldview by a clear separation of facts and values. The best knowledge is value-free, prescinding from ethics and its imperatives, scientifically objective. All we needed was Emmanuel Kant (1724–1804) to show us that we cannot really know things as they are in themselves. We can only reconstruct them in our minds. Modern science assimilated Kant's epistemology because it fits science's mechanistic, value-free, objective outlook that makes hypotheses, verifies them by their rationality and correspondence with evidence, organizes the hypotheses into theories, and puts the theories to work in industry and technology that dominate nature.

By the end of the seventeenth century, John Locke was able to state simply, knowing that it would be accepted easily, that God gave the world to man for him to exploit for his own convenience and benefit.[20] The stage was set for the rise of value-free technology, and for nature to be understood as "a collection of resources awaiting the plundering powers of the Euro-American peoples."[21]

Man-Against-Woman: Reformation Protestantism

Man's relationship with nature and his relationship with woman are themselves related. Man sees woman as embodying two principles: one acceptable and one unacceptable. The acceptable principle: woman as guardian of the hearth, keeper of the home and of the family, the one who watches over and nourishes law-abidingness, sexual purity, religion. The unacceptable principle: woman as unbridled sexuality, as subject to biological rhythms, as whimsical and therefore dangerous, as non-rational (scatterbrained, silly, lightheaded), as intuitive, as perceiving through love rather than with reason alone, as the embodiment of all that is disordered and dangerous in nature *as nature*.

As man's relationship with nature has, in the process of secularization, evolved into one of always greater domination of nature by man (as "master-slave" relationship), so too, by a kind of mutual causality, reciprocity, man has tended to put the unacceptable side of woman (woman insofar as he finds her unacceptable) in the same relationship. He tends to treat woman-as-nature *as nature*.

All this, of course, in the cultural perspective of the reformation, where nature is understood as fallen and under judgment. The male domination of and exploitation of nature, and of woman-as-nature, has, in part, religious (properly: Protestant reformation) roots. The biological fact is that, like nature as perceived by man, woman's body is ordered to others in a way that man's is not. For each of us, our mother's body and her whole daily routine were at one time completely at our command. Woman, much more than man, *is* nature.[22]

Moreover, reformation Protestant rejection of the Blessed Virgin Mary as venerated in Catholicism, and of the church as mother, has considerable cultural relevance regarding man's alienation from woman. The two-kingdom theology of the Protestant reformation, with its strong implications of man-against-nature, goes together with another even more central doctrinal element: the person's capacity, need, and call to go directly to the Father and to his Son Jesus without at all passing through the intermediacy of a mother, and in particular of a mother-church. Not that reformation Protestantism bypasses the church or the Christian community. But it does reject the church as mother. No Lutheran or Calvinist would ever refer to "Holy Mother Church" the way a Catholic or an Orthodox Christian might.

In Christian consciousness, the Blessed Virgin Mary stands for the church as mother. Mary stands for the church as mediating. A mother mediates the father's authority. Mary and the Catholic churches (Roman Catholic, Orthodox, Anglican) are mothers. These churches mediate doctrine through the interpretation of scripture and through tradition. They mediate God's power and mercy through the sacraments. They mediate his discipline and governance through church hierarchy.

Reformation Protestantism is masculine. It rejects both Mary and church as mothers of the new life in Christ. And it holds that new life comes from a male denominated source: the Father, through Jesus.

In Vatican II's *Dogmatic Constitution on the Church*, at the end of the chapter on the Blessed Virgin Mary, the council fathers speak of their joy and comfort that among their separated brothers and sisters some give due honor to the mother of the

Lord. This is especially true, the paragraph continues, of Christians of the Eastern (Orthodox) churches, "who with ardent devotion and devout mind concur in reverencing the mother of God, ever virgin."[23] More than a sisterly nod at similar churches, this statement indicates an important reality: those Christian churches that have relatively elaborate sacramental systems and highly developed organizational hierarchies give the same honor to the Blessed Virgin. And Christian churches pay honor to our Lady *to the degree* that they have sacramental systems and hierarchies.

The late Metropolitan Nicodeme of the Russian Orthodox Church once pointed out to me that the "feminine" churches, the churches that are true mothers, are the churches that most honor the mother of God. It seems logical and suitable that those Christians who hold less, according to the faith of their particular church, to the principles of sacramentality and mediated authority should have problems with all the reverence that Catholics and others have for Mary.

For example, in 1950 the reformation churches spoke out loudly in opposition to the papal definition of the dogma of the assumption of Mary into heaven. They threw out the baby's mother with the bath-water of papal infallibility, rejecting Mary as mother of Christians (in opposing the doctrine of the assumption), and rejecting the church as mother (in opposition even to the possibility of such an infallible definition of dogma). They rejected both mothers together, in complete accord with the faith presuppositions of their churches.

The idea of Mary as symbol of the church-as-mother is traditional. In Jungian psychology, Mary and the church as symbols both find their groundedness in the unconscious archetype of "the mother." And they frequently come together in Christian art and literature.[24] Teilhard de Chardin equates Mary and the church in the imagery of "the eternal feminine" which speaks, saying, "I am the church, the bride of Christ; I am the

Virgin Mary, mother of all humankind."[25] And Hans Urs von Balthasar, writing about the assumption of Mary's body into heaven, says, "This mother's body, already (in the overshadowing by the Spirit) a bride's body, is proleptically the church body from which and for which everything will be formed unto Christ, and which will later be called the church."[26]

Just *how* best to understand the church as feminine, as mother, is another question. Catholic understanding of the church's motherhood, especially in recent decades, seems to be moving in the direction of seeing the church as identified with the poor. Catholics increasingly understand the church as modeled by Mary, the woman of the Magnificat, in her temporal weakness and her femininity standing for the poor, the marginal, the rejected. The Catholic Church, thus, apparently understands herself increasingly as identified with the downtrodden, as a poor mother of the poor, like Mary the mother of Jesus. Reflections of this conception of the church as mother can be found in church teaching on her preferential option for the poor (understood as an identification with the poor), and even in the stands taken by the Holy See's delegations to international conferences.

Reformation Protestantism's rejection of the feminine in the two forms of the church-as-mother and Mary as mother-in-the-order-of-grace, filtered into general secular culture with its religious connections screened out, has contributed to a general rejection of the feminine and a demeaning of values generally considered feminine. Man-against-woman has become a dimension of Western culture. Reinforcing this rejection of the feminine has been an equal and parallel rejection of the feminine on the part of modern science.

Man-Against-Woman: Modern Science

Carolyn Merchant, in her study of women, ecology, and the scientific revolution, *The Death of Nature*, begins her book by saying that "women and nature have an age-old associa-tion—an affiliation that has persisted throughout culture, lan-guage, and history."[27] Nature has always been feminine, female, Mother Nature, Mother Earth. Fertile nature nurtures us and cradles us.

When Copernicus took mother earth from the center of the universe and replaced it with the masculine sun, nature and women both took a fall. With the scientific revolution, nature was perceived not as an ordered cosmos but as an unruly and disordered field for man to conquer, dominate, and use. And nature was generally perceived as female, as feminine.

Francis Bacon called nature "a common harlot," regularly referred to nature as female, and often used sexual imagery in speaking about science's conquest of nature. Bacon described nature as a fecund female slave; she and her children were to be brought into total submission by man and exploited by him. Bacon "provided the language from which subsequent gener-ations of scientists extracted a more consistent metaphor of lawful sexual domination."[28]

The expression of the subjugation of nature in sexual terms is not limited to words. As Rosemary Radford Ruether has put it, "the structures of patriarchal consciousness that de-stroy the harmony of nature are expressed symbolically and so-cially in the repression of women."[29]

The devaluation of woman can be explained at least par-tially by the fact that woman is seen as closer to nature than man. Her body and its functions seem closer to nature. The social roles that her body leads her into are also understood as closer to nature. And the psychic structure that comes from her body puts her, in cultural consciousness, closer to nature. Is this biological determinism? Of course not; in reality, woman is no closer to nature than man. But our culture *places* her closer to nature. She stands and falls with nature. And so man-against-nature includes man-against-woman.

Man Against Himself: Reformation Protestantism

Man's alienation from the natural world and his alienation from woman and from the feminine imply a third alienation, from himself. And because our Western culture has a strong male cast, all of us insofar as we share that culture also share in its alienation: from nature, from the feminine, from our own human nature.

Reformation Protestantism has not helped us; it has, rather, contributed heavily to our alienation from our human nature through the Lutheran doctrine of justification and the Calvinist theology of predestination. Floating now more or less free from their faith underpinnings, these teachings on justification and predestination take shape as attitudinal cultural elements: a pessimism and lack of respect toward human nature, and especially toward the poor and the marginal people of our own and other societies.

The Lutheran theology of the two kingdoms, and its rejection of the feminine especially in its maternal form, go together with Luther's understanding of human nature. Luther's doctrine of justification by faith alone holds the center of his entire teaching. The other side of the coin of the doctrine of justification is Luther's idea of human nature. Through original sin, human nature has utterly fallen, and lies, corrupted integrally and profoundly by sin, under God's divine judgment. Even after baptism, human nature remains quite corrupt, sinful, fallen. Its only salvation lies in the mercy of God brought to us by Jesus Christ.

Human will, for Luther, has no freedom; it is in bondage to sin unless and until God himself moves it in another direction through his Holy Spirit. God is all-powerful and governs all things in the universe. "There is thus a cosmic subjection to God's rule that shatters the pretensions of free choice."[30] In his *De servo arbitrio,* a hard and pointed response to Erasmus' *De libero arbitrio,* Luther writes: "Everything we do, everything that happens, even if it seems to us to happen mutably and contingently, happens in fact nonetheless necessarily and immutably, if you have regard to the will of God."[31] What God foreknows takes place of necessity.

Human nature is not only intrinsically bad, sinful, but—as it is individualized in persons—predestined. The Calvinist theology of predestination together with the notion that those predestined to heaven are also rightly and well rewarded in this life is only a step away from the conclusion that those who are less well-off, the poor and the marginal, are predestined to hell and not worthy of our respect.

How much of these ideas of fallen human nature and of the unworthiness of the lower classes has determined our culture? A great deal, I think; much that pits us against our own human nature. A culture that has little respect for human nature has little respect for human life. It can justify the killing of innocent human life by abortion, and even promote abortions among the less privileged classes and peoples. It can tolerate torture and denial of human rights as long as they do not take place at home. It can envisage nuclear war in the same way that it passed over in silence the World War II bombing of Dresden. It can and does look for the technological solution to human problems, of both persons and societies, without regard to the essential dignity of all human nature and of every person.

Man-Against-Himself: Modern Science

The mechanization of nature by modern science has included the mechanization of human nature. Real concern about the ethics involved in *in vitro* fertilization, in genetic engineering, and in computerized public access to private information, to take three examples, manifests the breadth and the gravity of contemporary problems that put us in conflict with our own human nature. Alienated from our own nature, we defeat ourselves by our technological solutions. The objective and value-free attitude of science has permeated our cultural attitude toward human nature.

We have taken as our unifying model for science, for society, and for the person: the machine. The machine-as-model has restructured human consciousness so completely that we do not question its appropriateness or its validity.

> Nature, society, and the human body are all composed of interchangeably atomized parts that can be repaired or replaced from outside. The "technological fix" mends an ecological malfunction, new human beings replace the old to maintain the smooth functioning of industry and bureaucracy, and interventionist medicine exchanges a fresh heart for a worn-out, diseased one.[32]

The mechanization of nature has meant the depersonalization of human nature. Human beings, depersonalized and mechanized, become objects of technological manipulation. They can be tested, broken by torture, scrutinized and analyzed, sterilized, drugged, killed, and created. They can be numbered and classified, manipulated individually and in small or large groups, repressed, steered, or terminated.

Theology's Strange Silence

In his monograph, *Teilhard in the Ecological Age,* Thomas Berry writes:

> In the modern Western world, the strange thing is the relative silence of Christian traditions in dealing with this basic issue of human relationships with the earth, a situation which is undoubtedly due to the strong emphasis on the redemption experience with relatively little concern for the functional processes of the created world.[33]

One sees how and why Berry's statement stands true of theology in the reformation tradition. There, in fact, the order of redemption and the order of creation have always held together only in a tension of contraries, in one way or another along the lines of Luther's two kingdoms and two regimes. But what about Catholic theology where, doctrinally, redemption and creation have always been seen as two facets of the one great reality of salvation?[34] What is true of Catholic faith no longer holds true of most Catholic theology. What happened?

Briefly, against Luther and Calvin, the Council of Trent (1545–1563) stressed the inherent goodness of the whole natural order, the order of creation. But, without reflection and certainly without intending it, Trent in its theology implicitly accepted the separation of the orders of creation and redemption. After Trent, the thought of Thomas Aquinas—completely integrative of creation and redemption—was transformed by his two greatest commentators, Francisco Suarez and Thomas Cajetan. They both distinguished a natural goal for human beings and a supernatural goal. And so they separated the creation (which they saw as belonging to the natural order) and redemption (belonging to the supernatural order).

The First Vatican Council took up the medieval scholastic expression, "creation from nothing." But Vatican I changed that idea from a metaphysical, "vertical" line of an existential relationship between creature and Creator to a "horizontal" idea. Now, "creation from nothing" has a new meaning: not a metaphysical relation in every creature by which the creature depends on the Creator for its existence, but an *action* of God at the beginning of history. Creation and redemption are separated.[35]

The Second Vatican Council put this right, in its *Pastoral Constitution on the Church in the Modern World,* using the general ideas of Teilhard de Chardin to show how creation and redemption are integrated, two aspects of one great process of salvation worked out in history. But Catholic theology has not yet caught up with Vatican II. Max Wildiers writes that "Catholic theology is in a critical period of transition. . . . We cannot speak of there being a consistent rethinking of Christianity within the framework of the modern world."[36] True. But Teilhard has given us an impetus and a basis for such a rethinking. And *The Pastoral Constitution on the Church in the Modern World,* following the lines of Teilhard's thought, has set a programmatic outline that Catholic theology has yet to follow up.

In this regard, the theology of, for example, Catholic theologian John-Baptist Metz does not differ from the theology of German authors in the reformation tradition like Wolfhart Pannenberg and Jurgen Moltmann. It stays focused on human history as eschatology, and it almost completely neglects personal relationship with nature in any form. In the same way, Latin American theology of liberation, while open to the study of person-nature relationships, has never come to grips with them. Like much Catholic theology today, it operates at the level of person, society, and history, but never at the level of human nature or of the natural world, nor even of human work, science, and technology. A notable exception like Rosemary Radford Ruether only proves the rule. Clearly and brilliantly within an authentic Catholic tradition, she treats our relationship with nature, emphasizing the social and political dimensions of that relationship.[37]

The failure of most Christian theology to seriously consider the human relationship with nature has unfortunate consequences. In general, contemporary systematic theology has failed to treat problems of human ecology, problems of man-woman relationships, and problems relating to human biology. The result: the neglect of whole areas that call out for theological reflection: genetics and genetic research, human sexuality, abortion, fertility control, human dying, the chemical manipulation of human nature, man-woman relationships, and the

whole ecological question. The systematic theologians have left
these fields to the Catholic moral theologians and the Protestant Christian ethicists. Most Protestant Christian ethics, however, finds itself stymied by the reformation tradition's
separation of salvation from the world of nature. And most
Catholic moralists remain obsessed by the question, "How far
can you go?"

But are not questions about the person-nature relationship
ethical questions? Yes, surely. But before they are questions of
ethical value, they are questions of *meaning* in the light of
Christian faith. Values follow from meanings. Meanings come,
in this case, from theological reflection. And this is what we
need.[38]

Pierre Teilhard de Chardin has already bequeathed to us
a great legacy. His religious thought overcomes the person-nature split. Teilhard rethinks our relationships, as persons, with
the whole natural order in terms of our relationship with God
in Jesus Christ risen. In so doing, he gives us a Christian vision
in which the orders of creation and redemption can be understood as two dimensions of the historical process of the recapitulation of all things in the risen Christ, and a vision in which
the loving universal influence of the risen Christ, together with
our own love for him and for all things in him, overcomes the
alienations of man-against-nature, man-against-woman, and
man-against-himself—a vision designed especially to show how
our alienation from God, and so from everything else including
ourselves, has been and is overcome in Jesus Christ.

Teilhard and the Person-Nature Relationship

Mary Evelyn Tucker has shown how Teilhard's vision can
provide the basis for an ecological spirituality: it can teach us
the meaning of human endeavor by showing us the personal in
the cosmos.[39] I agree, but I would go, following Teilhard himself, much further. The "personal" in the cosmos has a capital

"P." We can understand the world as personal because it finds its center and source of existence and forward movement in a Person, in Jesus Christ risen.

For Teilhard, the Christ of history is the center of the universe. Concerning the relationship between the risen Jesus and the world, Teilhard writes that these essential affirmations of Saint Paul sum up everything: "In him all things hold together" (Col 1:17), and "in him all things find their completion" (Col 2:10; see Eph 4:9), in such a way that "Christ is all things and in all" (Col 3:11).[40]

Vatican II's *Pastoral Constitution on the Church in the Modern World* repeats Teilhard when it states: "The Church . . . holds that in her most loving Lord and Master can be found the key, the focal point, and the goal of all human history."[41] Jesus centers the world on himself, risen and glorified. He stands at history's end, at the point of his second coming, the focal point and goal of all creation and of all that we are and do.

The risen Jesus' presence permeates everything; it shines at the heart of all things. "All around us," Teilhard writes, "Christ is physically active in order to control all things. . . . He ceaselessly animates, without disturbing, all the earth's processes."[42] The universal influence of the risen Jesus' love extends not only to every human heart but to the heart of the world and to every single part, every atom and molecule, every rock and breeze. His love holds all things together and moves them forward.

And so Jesus risen gives unity to all things. "All energies," Teilhard writes in a letter to Maurice Blondel, "hold together, are welded deep down into a single whole, and what the humanity of the Lord does is to take them up again and re-weld them into a transcendent and personal unity."[43] And so Jesus gives himself to each of us not only in our prayer and worship, not only in the Eucharist, but "through a world which is to reach completion even on a natural level by reason of its relationship to him."[44]

Teilhard, taking the incarnation seriously, sees that therefore matter is the proper vehicle of spirit and that all things are one, and are to be more one, in the risen Jesus Christ who loves each of us and all of us and the world, and who calls us to love him, to love one another, and to love the world itself. Love unifies, his love and ours. And, in him, love overcomes all alienation, from God, from one another, from ourselves.

We are, in Teilhard's vision of reality, one with nature, actively co-creating and building in Christ in love toward the future and, ultimately, toward the ultimate future.[45] We are one with the feminine. The feminine, for Teilhard, means "the spirit of union," an essential element of each of the dimensions of the universe: human, cosmic, Christic.[46] And we are one with ourselves because our human nature finds its dignity and value in the human heart of God who stands, in Jesus risen, at the heart and center of the life of the world and of the life of each one of us.[47]

Teilhard's spirituality of unification in Christ through love is, in itself, an ecological spirituality.[48] Even though the ecological crisis was not so evident in Teilhard's time, and he gave it no direct attention as such, his spiritual doctrine answers that crisis in giving us an ecological spirituality that transcends the person-nature split. And it goes further than ecology, presenting us with a Christian vision for life in the world.[49]

Notes

1. Here and throughout this chapter I deliberately use apparently sexist language, e.g., "man," to indicate, linguistically, predominantly male values in a predominantly male civilization. Rarely is "sexist language" appropriate, but here it seems to be.

I do not define "nature" and "person" clearly, since I want them to keep all their connotations. Their meaning here is understood in their use.

2. Vol. 155, n. 3767 (March 10, 1967), pp. 1203–1207, frequently reprinted—e.g., in F. Schaeffer, *Pollution and the Death of Man* (Wheaton, Illinois: Tyndale, 1970), Appendix.

3. White, in Schaeffer, *ibid.*, p. 111.

4. White, *ibid.*, p. 114.

5. Leo Marx, "American Institutions and Ecological Ideals," *Science*, 170 (1970), p. 948; Paul Ehrlich, *How To Be a Survivor* (New York: Ballantine, 1971), p. 129.

6. Max Nicholson, *The Environmental Revolution* (London: Hodder, 1969), p. 264.

7. "Ecology and the Death of Providence," *Zygon*, 15 (1980), p. 67.

8. Gen 1:26–28.

9. See H. Paul Santmire, *Brother Earth: Nature, God, and Ecology in Time of Crisis* (New York: Nelson, 1970); Joseph Sittler, *The Ecology of Faith* (Philadelphia: Fortress, 1970); Michael Hamilton (ed.), *This Little Planet* (New York: Scribner, 1970); Ian Barbour (ed.), *Science and Secularity: The Ethics of Technology* (New York: Harper, 1970); *idem* (ed.), *That Earth Might Be Fair* (New York: Harper, 1972); Christopher Derrick, *The Delicate Creation* (London: Devin-Adair, 1972); John Passmore, *Man's Responsibility for Nature* (London: Duckworth, 1974); Thomas S. Derr, *Ecology and Human Need* (Philadelphia: Fortress, 1975); Don E. Marietta, Jr., "Religious Models and Ecological Decision Making," *Zygon*, 12 (1977), pp. 151–166; Hugh Montefiore, "Man and Nature: A Theological Assessment," *Zygon*, 12 (1977), pp. 199–211; Rowland Moss, "God, Man, and Nature," *The Teilhard Review*, 13 (1978), pp. 89–103.

10. *Christ and Counter Christ* (Philadelphia: Fortress, 1972), p. 121.

11. *Ibid.*, p. 124. For two quite nuanced positions, see: Hans Schwarz, *On the Way to the Future* (Minneapolis: Augsburg Publishing House, 1972), pp. 127–130; Frederick Elder, *Crisis in Eden: a*

Religious Study of Man and Environment (Nashville: Abingdon, 1970), pp. 19ff.

12. Paul Santmire, *Metanoia,* special supplement to the June 1970 number, single page.

13. The classic reference for Martin Luther's two-kingdom concept is: "Temporal Authority: To What Extent It Should Be Obeyed" (1523), in Martin Luther, *Selected Political Writings,* ed. J. Porter (Philadelphia: Fortress, 1974), pp. 51–69. The "two-kingdom" discussion is situated within Luther's treatment of the modes of God's active ruling. The "two-kingdom" doctrine has been controversial among Lutheran theologians, especially in this century, mostly for the reasons I indicate in this chapter. See Eric W. Gritsch and Robert W. Jenson, *Lutheranism* (Philadelphia: Fortress Press, 1976), p. 179; Roy J. Enquist, "Two Kingdoms and the American Future," *Dialog,* 26 (1987), pp. 111–114. On Luther's ideas about human nature, see especially Jared Wicks, *Luther and His Spiritual Legacy* (Wilmington: Michael Glazier, 1983), pp. 124–153. Wicks shows the importance for living of Luther's dynamic and existential notion of fallen human nature. "Human nature" for Luther is not just a philosophical idea; it implies a whole program for Christian life.

14. See *Der Glaube der Christenheit,* 5th ed. (Göttingen: Vandenhoeck & Ruprecht, 1965), pp. 117–172; *Theologische Ethik,* vol. II, part I, 2nd ed. (Tubingen: Mohr, 1959), pp. 655–666. See also J. Wicks, "Justification and Faith in Luther's Theology," *Theological Studies,* 44 (1983), pp. 3–29.

15. Carolyn Merchant, *The Death of Nature* (San Francisco: Harper & Row, 1983), p. 164.

16. B. Farrington (ed.), *The Philosophy of Francis Bacon* (Liverpool: Liverpool University Press, 1964), p. 62.

17. Unpublished paper given at the Teilhard Conference, Wantage, Great Britain, 1984, p. 2.

18. Jane Mathison, *The Mirror of Nature,* unpublished lecture given at the Teilhard de Chardin Centre, London (December 13, 1983), p. 3.

19. *Ibid.,* p. 4.

20. "Second Treatise of Government," in P. Laslett (ed.), *Two Treatises of Government* (Cambridge: Cambridge University Press, 1963), Chapter V, sections 34–40.

21. Thomas Berry, "Religion, Ecology and Economics," *Teilhard Perspective*, 19 (1986), pp. 1–8.

22. See Walter Ong, *In the Human Grain* (New York: Macmillan, 1967), Chapter 11, "The Lady and the Issue," pp. 188–202; Ong's essay considers the Protestant rejection of the papal definition of the dogma of the assumption, a rejection he understands as associating "two apparently irrelevant things so often associated in separatist movements: resentment of authority and a desire to write Our Lady off the record" (p. 189).

It is not true, of course, that the Christian tradition outside of reformation Protestantism has been free from the devaluation of the feminine. Far from it. Thomas Aquinas and Augustine of Hippo are two famous cases in point among important writers, but the historical practice within the Roman Catholic, Orthodox, and Anglican churches could supply myriad examples. The Calvinist John Knox can cite Tertullian, Augustine, Ambrose, Paul, and John Chrysostom, among others, in his diatribe against women rulers (Geneva, 1558), stating that God has taken from woman "all power and authority, to speak, to reason, to interpret, or to teach . . . (or) to rule or to judge in the assembly of men" because God has given those "to man, whom he hath appointed and ordained his lieutenant on earth": *The First Blast of the Trumpet Against the Monstrous Regiment of Women on Earth,* quoted in *Not In God's Image,* ed. J. O'Faolain and L. Martines (New York: Harper & Row, 1973), p. 262.

23. No. 69; found in Walter M. Abbott (gen. ed.), *The Documents of Vatican II* (New York: America Press/Geoffrey Chapman, 1966), p. 96.

24. See Carl Jung, "Psychology and Religion," in *Collected Works of C. G. Jung,* trans. R. F. C. Hull, vol. II (New York: Pantheon Books, 1958), p. 71.

25. *Writings in Time of War,* trans. R. Hague (New York: Harper & Row, 1968), pp. 200–201.

26. M. Kehl and W. Löser (eds.), *The von Balthasar Reader,* trans. R. Daly (New York: Crossroad, 1982), p. 219.

27. *Op. cit.,* p. xv.

28. Evelyn Fox Keller, *Reflections on Gender and Science* (New Haven/London: Yale University Press, 1985), p. 34. See Merchant, *op. cit.,* pp. 164–190.

29. "Women, Ecology, and the Domination of Nature," *The Ecumenist,* 14 (1975), p. 5. Sherry B. Ortner tries to explain the devaluation of women in culture by examining what seems universal to every culture: the perception of woman as closer to nature than man is. I have used her ideas in the following paragraph; see "Is Female to Male as Nature Is to Culture?" in *Woman, Culture, and Society,* ed. M. Rosaldo and L. Lamphere (Stanford: Stanford University Press, 1974), pp. 70–87. Denise Lardner Carmody, on the other hand, contests that women are universally seen as closer to nature and *therefore* inferior (Japanese culture, she claims, places nature superior to culture!), and suggests that women's perceived closeness to nature can work significantly in their favor, an "at least potential badge of honor"; see *Feminism and Christianity* (Nashville: Abingdon, 1982), p. 148; cf. pp. 147–149.

30. Wicks, *art. cit.,* p. 19.

31. *Luther's Works, The American Edition* (St. Louis/Philadelphia: Fortress, 1955ff), vol. 33, p. 37, quoted in Wicks, *ibid.*

32. Merchant, *op. cit.,* p. 193.

33. Teilhard Studies No. 7 (Chambersburg, Pa.: Anima Books, Fall 1982), p. 20.

34. This is generally true also of Jewish, Anglican, and Orthodox doctrine.

35. See Robert Faricy, *Building God's World* (Denville, N.J.: Dimension, 1976), pp. 75–86.

36. *The Theologian and His Universe* (New York: Seabury, 1982), p. 215.

37. See, for example, her chapter on "Ecology and Human Liberation: A Conflict between the Theology of History and the Theology of Nature?" in her book *To Change the World (The Kuyper*

Lectures at the Free University in Amsterdam) (London: SCM, 1981), pp. 57–70.

38. I have tried to do some of this in *Wind and Sea Obey Him: Approaches to a Theology of Nature* (London: SCM, 1982).

39. *The Ecological Spirituality of Teilhard*, Teilhard Studies No. 13 (Chambersburg, Pa.: Anima Books, Spring 1985).

40. "My Universe," in *Science and Christ*, trans. R. Hague (London: Collins, 1969), p. 54.

41. "Introductory Statement," section 10, my translation.

42. "My Universe," *op. cit.*, p. 59.

43. Letter of February 2, 1916, in *The Making of a Mind*, trans. R. Hague (London: Collins, 1965), p. 93.

44. Letter of December 12, 1919, in H. de Lubac, "Maurice Blondel et le Père Teilhard de Chardin, mémoires échangés en decembre 1919, présentés par H. de Lubac," *Archives de philosophie*, 24 (1961), p. 154. Some persons seem to think that all Teilhard has to contribute to an ecological theology can be found in *The Phenomenon of Man*. Sean McDonagh writes: "We need a new story of the emergence of the earth and of the role of the human race within the community of the living, so that the human vocation to care for our earth—the garden planet of the universe—can be given a contemporary meaning. Many of the strands of this story have already been woven by Pierre Teilhard de Chardin in his book *The Phenomenon of Man*. A theology of creation based on this story could help to arouse us to the need to push back the web of death which is rapidly encircling the globe": *The Tablet* (15 November 1986), p. 225. The theology of creation, however, already exists in the published writings of Teilhard. See also, among more recent commentators on Teilhard in English, Ursula King, *Towards a New Mysticism* (London: Collins, 1980), especially Chapters 5, 6, and 9, pp. 104–143 and 192–218; J. A. Lyons, *The Cosmic Christ in Origen and Teilhard de Chardin* (Oxford: Oxford University Press, 1982), especially Chapters 6, 7, 8, and 9, pp. 89–210; Robert Faricy, *All Things in Christ* (London: Collins, 1981).

45. Theodosius Dobzhansky put it precisely when he wrote: "The point which he [Teilhard] stresses again and again is that we are

not to be passive witnesses but participants in the evolutionary process": *The Biology of Ultimate Concern* (New York: World, 1969), p. 137.

46. *Letters to Two Friends*, trans. R. Hague (London: Collins, 1968), pp. 212–213.

47. See Faricy, *All Things in Christ, op. cit.*, Chapter 1, "Love and the Heart of Jesus," pp. 13–31, which shows the place of the heart of the risen Christ and the role of love in Teilhard's thought.

48. Not everyone agrees. Allerd Stikker, in *Teilhard, Taoism, and Western Thought*, Teilhard Studies No. 15 (Chambersburg, Pa.: Anima Books, Spring/Summer 1986), feels that Teilhard's "focus on the decisive role of human progress in evolution made him unable to relate to the total system of the earth" (p. 11). Stikker thinks that, because Teilhard valued technology highly and considered nature at the service of human beings, he could not therefore appreciate nature and so cannot help us much regarding ecology. Thomas Berry, in *Teilhard in the Ecological Age*, op. cit., holds that Teilhard was "heir to the imperial tradition in human-earth relations, the tradition of human control over the natural world . . . a faithful follower of Francis Bacon" (p. 16), and therefore, because of his "imperialist attitude toward nature" (p. 19), that he does not give us sufficient elements for an ecological spirituality. Both Allerd Stikker and Thomas Berry seem to think that Teilhard has insufficient respect for nature. Stikker suggests that the Teilhardian vision incorporates the Taoist reverence for nature (p. 11). Berry thinks that "the subordination of the natural world to human dominion and exploitation" was "the position of Teilhard" (p. 16). He wants to rectify Teilhard's thought so that the basic norm for progress "would be, not the human, but the well-being and integral functioning of the earth community" (p. 26). See also: Berry, "Religion, Ecology and Economics," *art. cit.*, p. 7. See T. Berry, *Technology and the Healing of the Earth*, Teilhard Studies No. 14 (Chambersburg, Pa.: Anima Books, Fall 1985), for a fuller development of his ideas, mostly brilliant and stimulating, on ecology. Both Stikker (p. 11) and Berry (*passim*) hold Teilhard to be too anthropomorphic. Stikker finds Teilhard too optimistic as to tech-

nology (p. 11), and Berry finds Teilhard too aggressive toward nature in his appreciation of technology (pp. 25–26).

On the other hand, Christian spirituality teaches us to love and respect nature without elevating it (as do some Eastern philosophies and religions) to an equal level with humanity on the scale of existence. To raise nature to an equal dignity with humankind is far from Christianity. The accusation that Teilhard is too anthropomorphic for ecology forgets that Christianity itself is anthropomorphic because its founder is an anthropomorph. And, further, to belittle technology solves nothing. The problem is never technology, but what we do with it.

Both Stikker and Berry seem to want to shift Teilhard's thought, adapting it, in the direction of a nature mysticism. But Teilhard's mysticism is entirely Christian, and his vision of human union with nature is wholly Christ-centered.

49. Tad Peters writes: "The consensus is that we are currently in the final throes of modernity and that a postmodern consciousness is struggling to be born. The central element in this new consciousness is the concern for wholeness, for personal and cosmic integration. The issue for us is: Just how should we think theologically in response to this cultural shift?": *Dialog*, 24 (1985), p. 293. I have tried here to indicate an answer to that question.

3
Jesus and the World

The relationship between the triune Christian God and the created world holds an important place in the thought of both the founder of analytical psychology, Carl Gustav Jung, and the Jesuit priest-scientist, Pierre Teilhard de Chardin. Jung and Teilhard had some things in common. They were contemporaries: Jung died in 1961; Teilhard on Easter Sunday, 1955. The ideas of both have had more influence posthumously than during their lifetimes. And both were concerned, almost obsessed, with this century's search for unity, for wholeness, for a unified and coherent and integrated view of reality.

In their writings, both Jung and Teilhard, each according to his own particular viewpoint, see God as somehow needing the world. Not only does the world need God. God needs the world; he is incomplete without it. God and the world are in mutuality. This chapter has as its purpose: to juxtapose Jung and Teilhard regarding their views of the wholeness and the mutuality involved in the God-world relationship, to see how their ideas compare, and to draw some conclusions.

1. Jung: The Wholeness of Quaternity

Jung's Method

In his writings about religion, Carl Jung examines the psychological validity of religious symbols, looking for their psychological meaning. His method is empirical, based on his experience in treating patients with psychological problems, and on the data of mythical, religious, literary, and other cultural phenomena. He uses the data of his experience to arrive at hypotheses suitable as bases for use in therapy, in research, and in further reflection. Jung's interest lies in symbols; in the field of religion, he works with the religious symbols that he finds in people and in cultures.

He does not, of course, reduce God or the experience of God or religion to psychology. He does not study God, nor the experience of God; for one "cannot make anything except a conceptual distinction between God and the experience of God."[1] He does not study religion. Jung studies concepts, symbols, ideas about God and about the experience of God and about religion. "I am always coming up against the misunderstanding," he writes, "that a psychological treatment or explanation reduces God to 'nothing but' psychology. It is not a question of God at all, but of man's ideas of God. . . . These things are the proper study of psychology."[2]

Jung's method, generally scientific, concerned with arranging the data so as to form ordered series of hypotheses that give the best possible explanation of the data, is necessarily open-ended. His ideas are always subject to revision; this gives him, he writes, "the uncomfortable feeling that there is much in my exposition that still needs improvement."[3]

Regarding his methodology, Jung has been accused of gnosticism and of its exact opposite, agnosticism, of theism and of atheism, of mysticism and of materialism. In reply to charges, he has quoted from the *British Medical Journal,* "a source," he writes, "that would seem to be above suspicion": "Facts first and theories later is the keynote of Jung's work; he is an empiricist first and last." Jung adds, "This view meets with my approval."[4]

Therefore, when Jung speaks of Christ or of God or of the Blessed Virgin Mary, we must keep in mind that he speaks not of objective realities outside the human psyche, although he does not deny their existence outside our psyche. He is talking about symbolic expressions of unconscious archetypes. Christ, for Jung, is first of all a symbol of the archetype of the self. God is primarily a symbol of the unity of all reality. The Blessed Virgin Mary symbolizes the archetypes of the anima (the feminine side of the male psyche), the shadow (the unconscious "dark side" of the psyche), and the mother. For Jung, and psychologically, our faith in these entities is a projection of the symbols arising from our unconscious archetypes that seek expression in faith.

Jung, then, not a theologian but a psychologist, speaks of images, ideas, concepts, symbols, and psychic structures. He does not, however, deny that these psychological realities have real referents in the objective order outside the human psyche.[5]

According to Jung, we tend always to search for a unified view of reality, for an understanding of ourselves and the world around us that has unity, wholeness. This human drive toward a unified, holistic conception of reality comes from deep within us; it manifests itself as an archetypal form or mold that produces quadrate symbols in myths, art, dreams, fantasies, and rituals. Quaternity enters into our grasp of reality as a whole; we tend to perceive the totality of things as fourfold. "The quaternity is an archetype of almost universal occurrence," Jung writes in *A Psychological Approach to the Dogma of the Trinity;* "it forms the logical basis for any whole judgment."[6] Any such judgment or affirmation of some totality must have a fourfold aspect. There are always four elements, four winds, four seasons, four "corners of the earth," and so on. "The idea of completeness is the circle or sphere, but its natural minimal division is a quaternity."[7] The fourfold mandala is a quaternity. So is the central and unifying symbol of Christianity, the cross with its four arms.

Again, the conscious psyche has four basic functions: thinking, sensation, intuition, and feeling. The feeling function finds itself allied with the unconscious; when it is suppressed, the conscious suffers a lack of wholeness. Psychologically we perceive the wholeness of things as fourfold.[8] How strange, then, that Christianity's main doctrine seems only threefold, the doctrine of the Trinity.

The Trinity and Christ

Jung studies the data of Christianity's trinitarian dogma because the Trinity "is the central symbol of Christianity."[9] He cites some principal New Testament formulae: "The grace of the Lord Jesus Christ and the love of God and the fellowship of the Holy Spirit be with you"[10]; " . . . chosen and destined by God the Father and sanctified by the Spirit for obedience to Jesus Christ . . . "[11]; "Pray in the Holy Spirit, keep yourselves in the love of God, wait for the mercy of our Lord Jesus Christ unto eternal life."[12] He quotes the early Christian creeds. And then he proceeds to analyze the data to try to make maximum psychological sense out of it.

The Trinity, he finds, is an archetypal symbol. And the history of the doctrine of the Trinity presents itself as the gradual crystallization of an archetype that molds the anthropomorphic conceptions of father and son, of life, and of different persons into an archetypical and numinous figure, the "Most Holy Three-in-One."

Symbols, for Jung, are the best possible representations

of archetypal data. And they are the only conscious expressions of unconscious mental life that we have available. They serve as our underlying generators of ideas and as the transformers of creative instinctual energy.[13]

Christ is himself an archetypal symbol. The symbol of Christ corresponds to the archetype of the self. To be precise, the self is not exactly an archetype; or, at least, it is a quite special archetype. The symbols of the archetype of the self refer to the total personality—including the ego and the whole unconscious together with all the archetypes in the unconscious. The self embraces the whole person; it is the psychic totality of the individual, "a reflection of the individual's wholeness."[14] Therefore the self's symbols have a kind of completeness. They tend to appear when a person is alone, in solitude, in states in which the psyche gathers together its forces without any external interruptions—for example, in prayer, or in crises of loneliness.

In the development of Christianity, Jung says, the historical "Rabbi Jesus was rapidly assimilated by the constellated archetype; in this way Christ realized the idea of the self."[15] However, we cannot distinguish empirically between the symbol of the self and the idea of the image of God. The two ideas always appear blended together. So the self appears as synonymous with the interior Christ of the Johannine and the Pauline writings ("I live, not I, but Christ lives in me"[16]). And Christ appears as synonymous with God ("of one substance with the Father"), just as—Jung adds—"the atman appears as the individualized self and as the animating principle of the cosmos."[17]

Christ is the true image of God, the *imago Dei*. Jung quotes Origen: "The image of the invisible God is the Savior."[18] The Christian too is the image of God insofar as Christ dwells in him. The ambiguity of the phrase "image of God" illustrates the inseparability of the self, Christ, and God.

The story of Christ stands for the self-realization of the individual person. This is the goal of all psychological as well as biological development. Jung calls psychological self-realization "individuation." Individuation means "coming to selfhood" or "self-realization."[19]

However, because I can know myself only as an ego, and because the self—as a totality—is indescribable and indistinguishable from a God-image, therefore "self-realization—to put it in religious or metaphysical terms—amounts to God's incarnation."[20] Furthermore, individuation is the most difficult task I have, a heroic and even tragic task; it involves suffering, a true "passion" of the ego. Therefore, through the Christ-symbol, I can get to know the true meaning of my suffering: I am on the way to realizing my wholeness. As a result of the integration of conscious and unconscious, the ego enters the realm of the "divine," where it participates in "God's suffering." "The cause of the suffering is in both cases the same, namely 'incarnation,' which on the human level appears as 'individuation.' "[21]

The problem, psychologically, with the symbol of Christ is that it is not really complete. As symbol of the self, Christ is not sufficiently total. The dark side is lacking. Evil, in some form and in some way, is a part of the self; and evil has no room in the symbol of Christ, who is like us in all things—precisely except for sin.[22]

It does no good to object to Jung that Christ entered fully into the dark aspects of human existence through his complete *kenosis* even including death on a cross. Jung replies, "All that has nothing to do with the dark side of man. Christ is on the contrary the innocent and blameless victim without the *macula peccati*, therefore not really a human being who has to live without the benefit of the Virgin Birth and is crucified in a thousand forms."[23]

Jung understands the *macula peccati*, the "stain of sin," in

terms of the reformation theologies of original sin and its consequence: fallen human nature. And so Jung does not see how
Jesus can be completely human; his nature is not fallen, and so
not completely like ours. (It can be noted now that Teilhard de
Chardin, whose ideas will be considered later in this chapter,
does not have this problem, because of the quite different Catholic doctrine of original sin and its effect on human nature.
Catholic teaching holds that Christ's human nature is precisely
and completely the same as ours.)

The fundamental incompleteness of the Christ-symbol,
Jung finds, has been accentuated through historical development. The myth of the self-realization of God in human form
"remained unassailably vital for a millennium," Jung writes
late in his life, "until the first signs of a further transformation
began appearing in the eleventh century."[24] From then on,
symptomatic unrest and doubt has increased—until now we
have perceived the outlines of a universal catastrophe, first of
all a catastrophe in the realm of consciousness. The threat is
"giantism—in other words, a hubris of consciousness—in the
assertion: 'Nothing is greater than man and his deeds.' "[25] The
transcendence, the otherworldliness, of the Christian myth has
been lost, clouded over by pride. Lost with it is "the view that
wholeness is achieved in the other world."[26]

The problem that Jung finds with the symbol of Christ he
also finds with the symbol of the Trinity. There is no room for
a "dark side." Even more importantly, the Trinity as symbol
lacks wholeness because it is not a quaternity. To Jung, the fact
that the church has always violently resisted a quaternity in
God appears as quite odd—especially odd in light of the fact
that the symbol of the cross is itself unmistakably a quaternity.
The cross symbolizes God's suffering in his encounter with the
world.[27]

In spite of the church's resistance to a quaternity in God,
Jung finds a strong tendency to such a quaternity in the doc-

trine of the devil. The devil "fills out" the Trinity to a quaternity.

The Devil and Wholeness

In Christ's death on the cross, the devil—the "prince of this world"—vanquishes the God-man, in that very act "digging his own grave."[28] In our psychology, Jung finds, we understand the devil as quite powerful. He is the "adversary," the equal and opposite number of Christ. And so, in alchemy and in gnosticism, "the devil is the aping shadow of God."[29] For Jung, the devil somehow, symbolically, belongs in God. In Christianity, this idea originates with Origen's doubt concerning the devil's ultimate fate and possible salvation.[30] It now seems a long way off before the *deus absconditus*, the devil, finds official ecclesiastical integration into the divinity—to say the least.

Yet, evil in our time, Jung points out, has taken on enormous proportions. "The Christian world is now truly confronted by the principle of evil";[31] he finds this principle in the concrete first in Nazi Germany and later in Communist Russia.[32] Evil today is much more than a simple absence of good, a mere *privatio boni*. It is terrible, and we have to learn to deal with it psychologically.

However, at another level and in another way, the symbol of the Trinity can become, and has become, a quaternity, a wholeness, by assuming into itself a "fourth" who represents matter, darkness, the intractable, the unconscious. This "fourth" is the Blessed Virgin Mary.

In the Roman Catholic understanding, Jung finds, the devil does not make up a "fourth" to the Trinity. Rather, this fourth place is taken, at least to some extent, by the Blessed Virgin Mary, especially in the dogma of her bodily assumption into heaven. Jung writes, "I consider the Assumption as a cautious approach to . . . the integration of the fourth metaphys-

ical figure into the divine totality; . . . the devil is still outside."[33] And: "In a Catholic quaternity, the fourth would be
the Mother, 99-per-cent divine; the devil would not
count. . . ."[34]

Wholeness and the Mother of God

"Mary was the instrument of God's birth," Jung writes in
his analysis of the Trinity symbol, "and so became involved in
the trinitarian drama as a human being. The Mother of God
can therefore be regarded as a symbol of mankind's essential
participation in the Trinity."[35]

The problem of the non-quaternity of the Trinity symbol
became acute during the Middle Ages. The precise psychological problem of medieval culture with regard to the Trinity and
the Blessed Virgin was, according to Jung, "the exclusion, or
the very qualified recognition, of the feminine element, of the
earth, the body, and matter in general. . . ."[36] "Mary represents the earth, which is also the body and its darkness."[37]

As a result, in medieval art and poetry, the quaternity appears in the immediate relationship to the Trinity of the bridal
church and of the Queen of Heaven—"often," Jung adds, "it
is difficult to distinguish between the two."[38] And medieval
iconology "evolved a quaternity symbol in its representations
of the coronation of the Virgin and surreptitiously put it in
place of the Trinity."[39] This "fourth" signifies actualization,"
i.e., entry into the materiality of this world, a materiality ruled
by the prince of this world, the devil. For matter is the dia-
metrical opposite of spirit; it is the devil's true abode.[40] So
when the Virgin is somehow included in the symbol of the
Trinity, also—along with her—are included both matter and
evil (the "corrupting principle of the cosmos").[41]

The medieval pictures of the assumption and of the coronation of Mary as queen of heaven show a real psychological
need for quaternity in God, in the Trinity. This same psycho-

logical need was "responsible for elevating her to the position of mediatrix, corresponding to Christ's position as the mediator, with the difference that Mary only transmits grace but does not generate it."[42]

The Protestant reformation brought about an important change: the rejection of both the Blessed Virgin Mary and of the church as mother. Jung understands that "the Church is, in the fullest sense, a mother; we speak not only of Mother Church, but even of the Church's womb."[43] It was quite natural that, in reacting against the mother church of Rome, the reformation remove altogether the mother of God from the realm of the divine Trinity.

In those parts of modern culture heavily dominated by Protestant culture—especially in English-speaking and German-speaking countries—the lack of wholeness in both the Christ symbol and in the Trinity symbol (which completely lacks the "fourth" of the Blessed Virgin) is grave. The image of Christ has "changed, under the influence of evangelical Protestantism, into the personal Jesus, who in liberal rationalism, which abhorred all 'mysticism,' gradually faded into a mere prototype."[44] Jung continues in the same vein: "The disappearance of the feminine element, namely the cult of the Mother of God, in protestantism was all that was needed for the spirituality of the dogmatic image [of Christ] to detach itself from the earthly man and gradually sink into the unconscious."[45] When such great and significant symbols fall into oblivion, Jung points out, "they do not disappear from the human sphere, nor do they lose their power."[46] They continue to operate, in the unconscious, often in the form of personal or collective neurotic complexes.

Observing the modern psychological need for wholeness and so for the integration of the feminine in the form of a mother into the divine Trinity, to make it a quaternity, Jung in 1947 predicted the proclamation of the dogma of the assumption of the Blessed Virgin Mary into heaven.[47] And in 1950, Pope Pius XII stated the doctrine as a dogmatic definition.

The Assumption

"The *Assumptio Mariae*," Jung writes in 1948, "paves the way not only for the divinity of the Theotokos (i.e., her ultimate recognition as a goddess) but also for the quaternity."[48] And so the assumption dogma, by emphasizing the taking up to heaven not only of Mary's soul but of her body, makes "a dogmatic reality of those medieval representations of the quaternity."[49]

Jung is well aware that the proclamation of the dogma was motivated by "the religious need of the Catholic masses,"[50] the psychological need for a greater wholeness in the symbols of their faith. What the dogma has virtually produced, although of course not defined as such, is the Christian quaternity.[51] And Jung understands the dogma as having immense importance for everyone. He writes, "The only ray of light is Pius XII and his dogma, but people do not even know what I am referring to when I say this."[52] Although "in the Protestant and Jewish spheres the father continues to dominate as much as ever," at least "in the realm of Catholic dogma the Mother of God and the Bride of Christ has been received into the divine thalamus [bridal chamber] only recently, after centuries of hesitancy, and thus at least been accorded partial recognition."[53]

Behind all this stands the archetype of the mother.[54] In this context, Jung quotes the Dominican psychologist, Father Victor White, O.P., who strongly suggests that the "underlying motif" of the dogmatic definition of the assumption is not peculiarly Christian. "Rather would it seem to be but one expression of a universal archetypal pattern, which somehow responds to some deep and widespread human need, and which finds other similar expressions in countless myths and rituals, poems and pictures . . . all over the globe."[55] This is the same archetypal pattern, Jung writes, personalizing it as a feminine deity, "who at the Council of Ephesus in 431 imperiously announced her claim to the title of 'Theotokos' (God-bearer), as distinct from that of a mere 'Anthropotokos' (man-bearer) accorded her by the Nestorian rationalists."[56] For Jung, then, as he puts it in his own vocabulary, "the Virgin worship is itself a vestige of paganism, by which the Christian Church secured the entail of the Magna Mater, Isis, and others."[57]

And the "feminine deity" is rooted in the major archetype of the mother, present in the individual and in the collective unconscious. The archetype of the mother "is the place where the symbol of wholeness appears."[58] This lends to the figure of the mother that extraordinary fascination which characterizes the "Eternal Feminine." And therefore, Jung concludes, "woman appears as the true carrier of the longed for wholeness and redemption."[59]

At the risk of boring the reader by repetition, let me point out again that Jung's interest lies in the psychology of symbols. He considers religious realities and all the content of religious faith only at the level of symbol. He knows very well that Catholics do not really worship the Blessed Virgin any more than they worship Kali or Demeter. He is interested in this: that the Catholic devotion to Mary that is crystallized in the definition of the assumption has the same *symbolic* roots as does Hindu devotion to Kali and the ancient Mediterranean devotion to Demeter. The archetype is the same.

It should be further noted that Jung, as we all are, was strongly conditioned culturally. The descendant of a long line of German-speaking pastors of the Swiss Reformed Church, Jung breathed the Germanic Protestant reformation culture, along with the reformation rejection of the Catholic synthesis of nature and grace and, also, the reformation polarization of the "kingdom of God" and the "kingdom of the world." His culture, perhaps, blinded him to the possibilities of quaternity to be found in the dogma of the incarnation.

In the writings of the Catholic priest Pierre Teilhard de Chardin, we do find a quaternity fully in God by reason of the incarnation of God's Son—a quaternity that includes, by reason of the incarnation, the "dark side" of reality, the material, and the feminine.

2. Teilhard: The Unity of All in Christ

Teilhard's Method

In all his philosophical and religious writings, the method of Pierre Teilhard de Chardin is remarkably similar to that of Carl Jung. Like Jung, Teilhard uses a general scientific method. He gathers the relevant data and arranges it to form hypotheses that make as much sense as possible and that can bear fruit for future research and for more productive life. And he clusters his hypotheses to make general theories.[60]

The first step, his first general theory, consists of a generalized theory, almost a philosophy, of evolution. He uses the data of the sciences of evolution to develop an ordered set of hypotheses that considers evolution as taking place not only at a biological level but, after the advent of the human species, especially in human society—in the form of an always increasing socialization. This socialization produces societies always more highly organized and therefore in some way having an always higher level of cultural consciousness. Through a sometimes tenuous reasoning, Teilhard posits, as a part of the hypothesis that rounds out his theory of evolution, "a Personal Center of universal convergence."[61]

Teilhard de Chardin moves to a second level to work out a theoretical theology of Christ, a Christology, within the framework of his theory of evolution. Here, in his Christology, he incorporates the data of Christian revelation, the data of faith; he presupposes, at the entrance of this second level of his thought, a personal act of faith in Jesus Christ as Savior and in the truths of Christian revelation. So he differs in this respect from Jung in his treatment of Christian symbols; Teilhard, unlike Jung, lets his personal faith—in his case, the faith of a Roman Catholic—into his theory. His faith seeks to understand itself better, and so Teilhard embarks on a properly theological enterprise.

In his Christology, Teilhard identifies the "Personal Center of universal convergence" of his evolution theory with Jesus Christ risen as the future focal point of the world's forward movement in history. The "Personal Center" of Teilhard's theory of evolution is an extrapolation from present converging lines of societal evolution. "It remains by nature conjectural, it remains a postulate."[62] "We feel we must find some positive evidence upon which to base such disturbing extrapolations."[63] That positive evidence is Jesus Christ risen, as revealed in the church as a fact of faith.

Teilhard not only identifies the risen Christ as the future focal personal Center of convergent evolution. He reasons that such a Center must be active in all of history. Inasmuch as Christ is that Center, "he is seen to be attainable and inevitably present in all things."[64] And it was to become that Center that "it was necessary for him, through the travail of his Incarnation, to conquer and animate the universe."[65]

In this way, Teilhard wants to show how God and the world come together in Christ, how a fundamental mutual complementarity exists in and because of Jesus Christ. The risen Christ is the linchpin who gives to reality its unity, wholeness, oneness—in himself. In Christ, God is personally involved in the world. "God is completely other in nature than the world, and yet unable to dispense with it."[66] The world, then, can be understood as "a mysterious product of completion and fulfillment for the Absolute Being himself."[67] "God is entirely self-sufficient, and yet the universe contributes something that is vitally necessary to him."[68] God has "introduced us *in et cum mundo* [in and with the world] into the triune heart of his immanence."[69] The created world completes, "fills out," the trinitarian God. The idea is remarkably similar to Carl Jung's quaternity.

Teilhard's third methodological step takes him to a third level, that of Christian spirituality, of the theology of Christian life. He finds the chief religious problem of our time at this level: the problem of a lack of unity of vision, the difficulty of seeing God and the world as a totality. He calls it "the problem of the two faiths."[70] Teilhard describes "the psychological situation of the world today"[71] in the following way. On the one hand, we find an upsurge of humanist aspirations. "That upsurge is the new faith in the world. And on the other side there is the vision of a transcendent and loving pole of the universe; it is unswervingly upheld by Christian dogma but, to all appearances, more and more abandoned by the main stream of religion; and this is the ancient faith in God."[72] Surely, Teilhard goes on, the two faiths should somehow be not antagonistic but structurally complementary. "On one side, represented by modern humanism, we have a sort of neo-paganism, bursting with life . . . headless. On the other, in the form of christianity, we have a head in which the blood no longer circulates at the necessary speed."[73] On one hand, "a cone that has no apex; on the other, an apex which has lost its base; two detached parts . . . that clamor to be joined together."[74]

Because the personal Center of convergent evolution, the "God of the forward," is the same as the incarnate traditional "God of the upward," Jesus Christ, the Christian can therefore understand the world as one in Christ. He can see the totality of reality as a unity, as a whole centered in the risen Christ. And he can love Christ and the world with one all-embracing love. The forward component of faith in the world and commitment to this-worldly matters, and the upward component of worship and love of God, come together in Jesus Christ. The horizontal vector and the vertical vector of the life of the Christian today come together in synthesis in a unitary and unifying vision of the wholeness of reality centered in the risen Christ.[75]

Creation and Redemption in Christ

In his Christology, Teilhard rethinks the traditional dogmas of creation and redemption. He wants to reformulate the doctrines of creation and redemption in more contemporary terms, in terms of a world and a human society in evolution toward a future focal center of convergence, Jesus Christ risen.

In an essay entitled "My Fundamental Vision,"[76] Teilhard situates his theology of creation in a trinitarian framework. He begins by saying he wants to use a theory of union instead of the old theory of being; he then defines being in terms of union: "to be" means "to unite" or "to be united."[77]

Teilhard supposes a triune God who contains his own trinitarian self-opposition and who exists by uniting himself—so making himself triune. "By the very fact that he unifies himself upon himself in order that he may exist," Teilhard continues, "the First Being *ipso facto* stimulates the outbreak of another type of opposition, not in the core of his being, but in the very opposite pole from himself."[78] This "other type of opposition" is the created world, a fruit somehow of God's own existence. The created world "emerges as a sort of echo or symmetrical response to Trinitization. It somehow fills a gap; it fits in."[79]

The world, then, is not something that God can just do without. On the contrary, he has freely willed to need it. So the world is not utterly contingent, and its creation is not an arbitrary act on God's part. God does not stand aloof from the world; he is not indifferent to what he has created; he is personally involved in the world, mutual with it.

Teilhard wants to avoid the "Great Watchmaker" idea of creation—as though God created the world the way a craftsman makes a watch, then winds it so it can run by itself. But Teilhard has to face the theological problem of God's freedom. He answers this problem by saying that in such deep waters, we cannot clearly distinguish between supreme necessity and supreme freedom. It seems to us that God creates necessarily, or at least inevitably. But we know he creates freely by the sure sign of the love with which he acts.[80] Action done in love is always done freely.

All this said, it remains that for us the Trinity appears to inevitably give rise to, create as a kind of extension of itself outside itself, what Jung calls "a fourth." Once again, we have a quaternity. The "fourth" is the created world.

The point of using a theory of union (instead of a theory of being) is this: Teilhard wants to rethink the traditional Christian doctrine of creation in New Testament terms—in particular, according to the Pauline and Johannine notion of "creation in Christ." And he sees that, to do this, he needs to think not in terms of being but in terms of union. So he considers creation as union. Notice that Teilhard wants to find a new way to *conceptualize* the doctrine of creation. He has no intention at all of changing the basic doctrine. He wants to bring its formulation more into line with the New Testament data—in other words, to make a better hypothesis.

To create means to unite. Creation itself is a process, and its expression in historical time is evolution. Evolution "is the expression of creation, for our experience, in time and space."[81] God "creates by uniting."[82] And God's act of creation, perceived by us as a process effecting the created world in historical movement, aims at the focal point of the world's movement: Jesus Christ risen. Christ is he "in whom everything is created and he in whom the entire world in all its depth, its length, its breadth, its grandeur, its physical and its spiritual qualities, comes to be and takes on consistence. . . . The world is above all a work of continuous creation in Christ."[83]

This is, of course, the Pauline idea of creation in Christ and of the reconciliation and the recapitulation of all things in Christ, expressed by Teilhard within an evolutionary thought-frame. The world, in history, is being more and more created as it converges on its future focal center, Christ, toward the world's end, death, and transformation when everything will be centered on Christ and God will be all in all. To use a Jungian vocabulary, the world together with all in it is being drawn always more—in and through Christ—into the Trinity to make a quaternity; the world, in and through Christ, is a "fourth" to the Trinity.

Furthermore, we too can steep ourselves in God's creative action, unite our own efforts to God's creative action so as to become "not only its instrument, but its living extension."[84] We contribute by our activity, in union with God's will, to the world's forward movement and so to its creation by whatever we do that is positive, that unifies or unites in any way. Since love is the great unifier, whatever we do in love participates in the Creator's action toward reconciling, uniting, all in Christ. In other words, we can understand our own efforts in the world as contributing to wholeness, to ultimate unity—as, so to speak, moving us into God in Christ (to use the Jungian words again, as moving us further into the "fourth" of the Trinity, into a quaternity—in Christ—with God).

And so we share too in Christ's work of redemption. Teilhard sees creation and redemption as two aspects of one great process of the recapitulation of all things in Christ. "Understood in their full sense," he writes, "creation, incarnation, and redemption are not facts which can be *localized* at a given point in time and space; they are true dimensions of the world."[85] In the context of redemption, Teilhard works out a theory of evil, including sin, as the antithesis of the unity and the unification that love produces.

Evil and Unification

Where does the process of creation as unification begin? And with what? Creation begins with a (hypothetical) infinite multiplicity at the antipodes of that pole of self-subsistent being that is God. "The multiple," Teilhard explains, "the *pure* multiple (with full emphasis on *pure*), or creatable *nil*, which is nothing . . . nevertheless . . . is a possibility of being."[86] In order for creation to happen, for God "to launch his attack on the multiple, God is forced inevitably into war with evil, 'the shadow of creation.' "[87]

Like Jung, Teilhard finds inadequate the idea of evil as merely a privation of good. He sees evil, rather, as an absence of oneness where unity should exist—as a lack of due unity. And if creation is understood as a long process of unification of the multiple, headed toward the unification of all things in Christ, this explains the problem of evil. "There can be no *order in the process of formation* which does not at every stage imply some *disorder*."[88] Through a gradual process (creation) of attracting elements to himself, drawing them into a unity in and toward Christ, the Creator builds up the world. At first, the unities that appear are quite simple. Later in evolutionary time they become more organized. Finally, the human species appears. And the process continues, especially in human society.

In this kind of process, every success is paid for by a certain amount of failure, waste, and breakage. In non-living things we find this failure as decomposition and disharmony, among living things as suffering and death, and, at the level of moral choice, as sin.[89] Evil is the "shadow which God inevitably produces simply by the fact that he decides on creation."[90]

A universe in evolution is necessarily "a universe which labors, which sins, which suffers. . . . Statistically, at every degree of evolution, we find evil always and everywhere, forming and reforming implacably in us and around us."[91] This evil includes sin as one of its types or forms. Sin is the deliberate movement of the will away from unity and from the loving that creates unity. "There is *only one evil*" for Teilhard: "disunity. We call it 'moral evil' [sin] when it affects the free zones of the soul."[92]

In this perspective, Teilhard can understand the suffering and death of Jesus on the cross as a struggle against evil, and—especially—as the victory over all evil, not only over sin but over death and every kind of evil. Moreover, the incarnation itself is seen as "the plunging of the divine unity into the ultimate depths of the multiple. . . . For Christ to make his way into the world by any side-road would be incomprehensible. . . . It is because Christ was 'inoculated' in matter . . . that he is so engrained in the visible world that he could henceforth be torn away from it only by rocking the foundations of the universe."[93]

Christ's death on the cross was a continuation of his descent into the multiple begun at his incarnation. The cross when "seen on the panoramic screen of an evolutive world . . . takes on a new importance and beauty. . . . Christ, it is true, is still he who bears the sins of the world; moral evil is in some mysterious way paid for by suffering."[94] Even more fundamentally, Christ "structurally in himself, and for all of us, overcomes the resistance to unification offered by the multiple resistance to the rise of spirit inherent in matter."[95] Christ bears the burden of creation. Without ceasing to be he who bears the sins of the world, and even "precisely as such," Christ is becoming more and more in our age "he who bears and supports the weight of the world in evolution."[96]

Teilhard summarizes in a sentence his view of the relationship between creation and the redemptive act of the cross: "If to create is to unite (evolutively, gradually) then God cannot create without evil appearing as a shadow—evil which has to be atoned for and overcome."[97] And he adds, "The cross is the symbol and the significant act of Christ raising up the world with all its burden of inertia. . . . Creation belongs in the category of effort."[98]

In this life, we live in the structure of the cross. And in Christ crucified each of us "must recognize his own true image. . . . The truth about our position in this world is that *in it we are on a cross*."[99] And the cross stands as the symbol of "the creative but laborious effort of humankind climbing toward Christ who awaits it."[100] The cross stands for "progress and victory won through mistakes, disappointments and hard work."[101] Teilhard describes the meaning of the cross in our lives in a poetic passage from *The Divine Milieu:*

> Toward the peaks, shrouded in mist from our human eyes, whither the cross beckons us, we rise by a path which is the way of universal progress. The royal road of the cross is no more nor less than the road of human endeavor supernaturally righted and prolonged. Once we have fully grasped the meaning of the cross, we are no longer in danger of finding life sad and ugly. We shall simply have become more attentive to its barely comprehensible solemnity.[102]

It is, then, not just the world, in and through Christ, that enters as a Jungian "fourth" into the Trinity to form a quaternity. It is the world with all its multiplicity, its resistance to creative unification, its physical and psychological and moral evil. And we too, with the world and with its evil, in and through Christ, enter into God to form a quaternity—for we really share in the process of creation, and we really share in the cross of Jesus. Finally, just as Carl Jung finds quaternity in the cross, Teilhard sees it as the symbol of unification, of wholeness.

We have seen that, for Jung, the Blessed Virgin Mary has an important symbolic role, especially in the dogma of her assumption, with regard to the wholeness of reality. What place does she have in the thought of Pierre Teilhard de Chardin? The next chapter tries to answer this question.

Notes

1. *Brother Klaus* (book review), in *Collected Works of C. G. Jung* (hereafter referred to as CW), Bollinger Series XX, tr. R. F. C. Hull (New York: Pantheon Books), vol. 11 (1958), p. 317. On Jung's psychological interpretation of Christian doctrine, see the important study of Clifford A. Brown, *Jung's Hermeneutic of Doctrine: Its Theological Significance* (Chico, California: Scholars Press, 1981); Brown makes it clear that Jung's method is unequivocally *psychological*.

2. *A Psychological Approach to the Trinity*, CW 11, p. 163, footnote 16. Jung has been described as Kantian in his method; see Adrian Cunningham, "Jungian Psychology," *A New Dictionary of Christian Theology* (London: SCM, 1983), pp. 311–312. A basically Kantian epistomology underlies all scientific method, in which data are gathered and then arranged to form hypotheses which, ordered, compose a theory. The theory *represents* the reality which remains in itself, true to Kant's philosophy, untouchable by our knowledge. Pierre Teilhard de Chardin's thought has the same Kantian cast.

3. *Ibid.*, p. 110.

4. *Religion and Psychology: A Reply to Martin Buber*, CW 18, pp. 663–664.

5. Cf. especially *Jung and Religious Belief*, CW 18, pp. 723–744.

6. *Ibid.*, p. 167; cf. *The Practice of Psychotherapy*, CW 16, p. 207: "The quaternity . . . is like the crossed threads in the telescope of our understanding."

7. *Ibid.* Cf. Jung's treatment of quaternity in reference to religion in *Jung and Religious Belief*, CW 18, pp. 713–717.

8. In William Blake's division of visions into four categories, the fourfold vision holds the highest place:

> Now I a fourfold vision see,
> And a fourfold vision is given to me;
> Tis fourfold in my supreme delight. . . .

Cf. *Poems from Letters*, iv, lines 83–88 (Oxford: Clarendon Press, 1923), p. 309. See the editors' analysis of Blake's classification of visions in D. J. Gloss and J. P. R. Wallis, editors, *The Prophetic Writings of William Blake*, vol. II (Oxford: Clarendon Press, 1926), pp. 21–50.

Interestingly enough, contemporary physics finds there to be four fundamental forces underlying all material reality: the nuclear (or strong) force, the weak force, the electromagnetic force, and the gravitational force.

9. *Ibid.*, p. 110.

10. 2 Cor 13:14.

11. 1 Pet 1:2.

12. Jude 20–21.

13. For an excellent and concise description of the main Jungian terms and concepts, see Michael Fordham, *Jungian Psychotherapy* (New York: John Wiley and Sons, 1978), pp. 3–10. See also Wallace B. Clift, *Jung and Christianity* (New York: Crossroad, 1982), pp. 1–78, for a masterfully clear exposition of Jung's ideas.

14. CW 11, p. 156.

15. *Ibid.*

16. Gal 2:20.

17. CW 11, p. 156.

18. "*Imago autem Dei invisibilis Salvator*," writes Jung, quoting the Latin of Migne, *P. G.*, vol. 12, col. 107 (*Selecta in Genesim*, IX, 6) in CW 9, vol. 2, Aion (1959), p. 37.

19. *Two Essays on Analytical Psychology*, CW 7, p. 171.

20. CW 11, p. 157.

21. *Ibid.*

22. Cf. Heb 4:15.

23. *Jung and Religious Belief*, CW 18, pp. 717–718.

24. *Memories, Dreams, and Reflections,* tr. R. and C. Winston (New York: Pantheon Books, 1963), p. 328.

25. *Ibid.*

26. *Ibid.*

27. *A Psychological Approach to the Dogma of the Trinity,* CW 11, p. 170. It also symbolizes the struggle of all who find themselves on the road to wholeness; cf. *The Practice of Psychotherapy,* CW 16, p. 262.

28. *Ibid.*

29. *Ibid.,* p. 177.

30. *Mysterium Conjunctionis,* CW 14 (1963), p. 188.

31. *Memories, Dreams, Reflections, op. cit.,* p. 328.

32. "Evil today has become a visible Great Power" (*ibid.,* p. 331).

33. *Jung and Religious Belief,* CW 18, p. 714.

34. *Ibid.,* p. 712.

35. *A Psychological Approach to the Dogma of the Trinity,* CW 11, p. 161.

36. *Psychology and Religion,* CW 11, p. 72.

37. *Ibid.,* p. 71.

38. *Ibid.*

39. *A Psychological Approach to the Dogma of the Trinity,* CW 11, p. 170.

40. *Ibid.*

41. *Ibid.*

42. *Mysterium Conjunctionis,* CW 14, p. 176.

43. *Two Essays on Analytical Psychology,* CW 7, p. 103.

44. *Answer to Job,* CW 11, p. 361.

45. *Ibid.*

46. *Ibid.*

47. In *A Psychological Approach to the Dogma of the Trinity,* published in German in 1948, CW 11, p. 170.

48. *Ibid.,* p. 170.

49. *Mysterium Conjunctionis,* CW 14, p. 186.

50. *Ibid.*

51. *Ibid.,* p. 188.

52. *Memories, Dreams, Reflections, op. cit.,* p. 332.

53. *Ibid.*, p. 201. Jung refers here to the wording of the Apostolic Constitution *Munificentissimus Deus* (Pius XII defining the assumption in 1950), section 22: "The place of the bride whom the Father had espoused was in the heavenly courts." Section 33: ". . . on this day the Virgin Mother was taken up to her heavenly bridal-chamber." Cf. *Jung and Religious Belief*, CW 18, p. 742.

54. Note that the archetypes (the shadow, the anima and animus, the mother, the child, the spirit, certain processes such as rebirth, and—in an enlarged sense—the self) are not symbols; they are, rather, unconscious molders, flexible die patterns for casting the metal of the psyche into symbols.

55. Quoted in *Mysterium Conjunctionis*, CW 14, p. 186, from "The Scandal of the Assumption," *Life of the Spirit*, V, p. 200.

56. *Mysterium Conjunctionis*, CW 14, pp. 186–187.

57. *Psychological Types*, tr. H. G. Baynes (London: Rutledge and Kegan Paul Ltd., 1923), p. 290.

58. *Answer to Job*, CW 14, p. 356.

59. *Ibid.*

60. Teilhard outlines his method in "Some Reflections on the Conversion of the World," *Science and Christ*, tr. R. Hague (London: Collins, 1969), pp. 122–123; also in "La pensée du Père Teilhard de Chardin," *Les études philosophiques* 10 (1955), pp. 580–581; and in "Un sommaire de ma perspective phénoménologique du monde," *ibid.*, pp. 569–571.

61. "Some Reflections on the Conversion of the World," *Science and Christ, op. cit.*, p. 122.

62. "The Christic," *The Heart of Matter*, tr. R. Hague (London: Collins, 1978), p. 91.

63. "My Universe," *Science and Christ, op. cit.*, p. 53.

64. *Ibid.*, p. 54.

65. *Ibid.*

66. "Action and Activation," *Science and Christ, op. cit.*, p. 182.

67. "The Heart of Matter," *The Heart of Matter, op. cit.*, p. 54.

68. "Christianity and Evolution," *Christianity and Evolution*, tr. R. Hague (London: Collins, 1971), p. 177.

69. "My Universe," *Science and Christ, op. cit.*, p. 56. See Chris-

topher F. Mooney, S.J., *Teilhard de Chardin and the Mystery of Christ* (New York: Harper and Row, 1966), pp. 174–176; Robert Faricy, S.J., *Teilhard de Chardin's Spirituality of the Christian in the World* (New York: Sheed and Ward, 1967), pp. 115–118.

70. See especially "The Heart of the Problem," *The Future of Man*, tr. N. Denny (London: Collins, 1964), pp. 260–269; "What the World Is Looking For from the Church of God at This Moment," *Christianity and Evolution, op. cit.*, pp. 212–220.

71. "Christianity and Evolution," *Christianity and Evolution, op. cit.*, p. 175.

72. *Ibid.*

73. *Ibid.*

74. *Ibid.*, p. 176.

75. Teilhard draws a diagram with a vertical vector and a horizontal vector and the diagonal resolution-vector of faith-vision and faith-adherence to Christ: "The Heart of the Problem," *The Future of Man, op. cit.*, p. 269.

76. *Toward the Future*, tr. R. Hague (London: Collins, 1975), pp. 163–208.

77. *Ibid.*, p. 193.

78. *Ibid.;* translation my own, since the official translation is theologically inadequate.

79. *Ibid.*, p. 195.

80. *Ibid.*, p. 194.

81. "Man's Place in the Universe," *The Vision of the Past*, tr. J. Cohen (London: Collins, 1967), p. 231.

82. "My Universe," *Science and Christ, op. cit.*, p. 45.

83. "Intégration de l'homme dans l'univers," unpublished lecture notes, 1930, lecture 4, pp. 12–13.

84. *The Divine Milieu*, tr. B. Wall, *et al.* (London: Collins, 1960), p. 64.

85. "Some General Views on the Essence of Christianity," *Christianity and Evolution, op. cit.*, p. 135.

86. "My Fundamental Vision," *Toward the Future, op. cit.*, p. 194; see "Christology and Evolution," *Christology and Evolution, op. cit.*, pp. 79–86.

87. *Ibid.*, p. 196.

88. *Ibid.*, p. 197.

89. *Ibid.*, pp. 197–198.

90. "Christology and Evolution," *Christology and Evolution, op. cit.*, p. 84.

91. *The Phenomenon of Man*, tr. B. Wall (London: Collins, 1965), p. 313.

92. "My Universe," *Science and Christ, op. cit.*, p. 80, footnote 15.

93. *Ibid.*, pp. 60–61.

94. "Christology and Evolution," *Christology and Evolution, op. cit.*, p. 85.

95. *Ibid.*

96. "Introduction to the Christian Life," *Christianity and Evolution, op. cit.*, p. 163; "He bears the whole weight of a world in progress," "Christianity and Evolution," *ibid.*, p. 171; see *The Divine Milieu, op. cit.*, p. 104.

97. "Some General Views on the Essence of Christianity," *Christianity and Evolution, op. cit.*, p. 135.

98. *Ibid.*

99. "Cosmic Life," *Writings in Time of War*, tr. R. Hague (London: Collins, 1967), p. 67.

100. "Intégration de l'homme dans l'univers," *op. cit.*, p. 13.

101. "Introduction to the Christian Life," *Christianity and Evolution, op. cit.*

102. *Op. cit.*, pp. 103–104.

4
God and the Feminine

The "Eternal Feminine"

In 1918, during the period in which Teilhard de Chardin wrote his first series of essays which set out, often in a somewhat poetic form, the themes of his later religious writings, he wrote a prose-poem, in the style of the Old Testament wisdom literature, on the "feminine" component of reality and the Blessed Virgin Mary: "The Eternal Feminine."[1] It is clear from this essay, from his letters and his retreat notes, and from a few paragraphs at the end of the 1950 essay, "The Heart of Matter," that Teilhard regarded the "eternal feminine" not as an abstract principle primarily, but—in the first instance—as a universal principle *concretized* in individual women, in the church as bride and mother, and in a particular and almost primordial way in the Blessed Virgin Mary. In his retreat notes, he writes of "the universalization of Our Lady."[2] And yet, the feminine, precisely as concretized in women, and especially in the mother of God, and in the church, symbolizes for Teilhard certain qualities of the whole cosmos: materiality, darkness, mystery.

"The Eternal Feminine," in Teilhard's 1918 essay with that title, speaks: "When the world was born, I came into being. . . . God instilled me into the initial multiple as a force

of condensation and concentration. In me is seen that side of
beings by which they are joined as one . . . along their road to
unity. . . . I am the essential Feminine.''[3] The Eternal Feminine, then, symbolizes creation through unification, the forward and upward spiritualization of the multiplicity inherent
in matter, a spiritualization through organization, unification,
"concentration." Briefly, the Eternal Feminine stands for creation in process. Later, the same voice says, "The more, then,
I become Feminine, the more immaterial and celestial will my
countenance be."[4] Matter tends, through the unifying effect of
progressive creation, toward spirit.

Finally, "I am the Church," says the Eternal Feminine,
"the bride of Christ." And, "I am Mary, the virgin, mother of
all humankind."[5]

Henri de Lubac has pointed out that, for Teilhard, the
eternal feminine in this essay is not an allegorical figure, she is a
"concrete universal": "it is not an abstract principle which is
personified in the Virgin—it is the Virgin, existing in her own
individuality, who is universalized in the principle."[6] The conclusion of the essay reveals the Blessed Virgin Mary to have been
the subject, the speaker, from the beginning. The Eternal Feminine of the essay is not, then, a personalization; she is, although
in a veiled way for most of the essay, the mother of God. Mary,
for Teilhard, is a concrete universal, a real and personal symbol
of the Eternal Feminine, of all women and all femininity, of
matter and of the creative forces that organize matter and move
it toward spirit. And so, in his personal retreat notes, Teilhard
can call Our Lady "the soul of becoming."[7]

More than an archetype, Mary nonetheless, as symbol,
corresponds to an archetype—in fact, to more than one archetype. Revealingly, Teilhard dedicates "The Eternal Feminine": "To Béatrix." In his pre-notes for the essay we find the
(eventually unused) title for a prologue to the essay: "Before a
Veiled Virgin: to Béatrix."[8] "Béatrix" is the "Veiled Virgin,"

who of course is the Blessed Virgin Mary. And, also, the name Béatrixes refers to Dante's Beatrice. John A. Sanford argues that Beatrice clearly is a projection of Dante's anima, that Dante projected his anima onto the person of Beatrice, and then "turned his encounter with the anima, which had fallen on Beatrice, into hard and creative work, and it kept him going for a lifetime."[9] There seems little doubt that Teilhard projected his anima on the Virgin Mary, at least in this essay. And he seems to have projected it onto other "Béatrixes." In later years, rereading a brief note he had once written on "The Feminine," Teilhard wept uncontrollably at the memory of all the reproachful "Béatrixes" he was sure he had hurt unwittingly in the past.[10]

If the "Veiled Virgin" of "The Eternal Feminine" symbolizes Teilhard's anima—and so the anima as an archetype of the collective unconscious—she also stands for the archetype of the mother. In an earlier essay, Teilhard calls Mary "the true Demeter."[11] Therefore Mary, while remaining for Teilhard a concrete universal, can be the church, and Mother Nature, and every type of mother.

The Assumption

Teilhard disagreed with Jung's opinion that the then increasing importance of Mariology in Catholic thought and devotion was due to women who sought better representation in the kingdom of heaven. He cites the history of spirituality to show that those with the greatest devotion to Mary have been men, and he underlines the strong Christian need to correct an overly masculinized idea of God as legitimizing the development of the cult of Mary; in fact, he himself had great personal devotion to Mary.[12]

He clearly believed in the dogma of the assumption and supported Rome's definition of that dogma. Nevertheless, he was unhappy at the way the dogma was presented, as can be seen from a letter to his good friend, Pierre Leroy, S.J.:

> I have read about it [the papal definition of the dogma of the Assumption] in the newspapers. . . . I spend my time in letter-writing and in conversations in answer to the S.O.S.'s that come to me from all sides. In fact, except for the small annoyance of having to show people how to "interpret" such authoritative statements, the famous document leaves me quite calm. Yelling out will not stop the world from turning. Still, what bothers me is to see that, although what Rome wants—to emphasize the Marian aspects, to keep dogma from evaporating into mere symbolism, to keep a certain primacy and a certain unity in the concept of humankind—is entirely correct, still it should be expressed differently. Not because of a simple question of words. But because of a *question of the World*—because the world has acquired a new dimension or organic genesis—and such a growth in dimensions completely transforms ideas (in their meaning) (even though the encyclical denies it): a sphere is not a circle! I wonder if a good psychoanalyst could not discover clear signs of a specific religious perversion: sado-masochism of orthodoxy—pleasure in swallowing or in making others swallow the truth in its most gross and bestial forms. But maybe I'm being a little unkind.[13]

Other letters of the same time show that Teilhard regarded the definition of the assumption as an act of "blind conservatism," and "somewhat of a challenge to physics and biology."[14] "I believe I see," he writes, "what is in the mind of the Roman theologians, and I agree with them. But their views are expressed in the most impossible language. . . . The most funny consequence of the Assumption's dogma is that, by its mere affirmation, the fundamentalists express the view that the dogma is *still evolving* (since there is not a word of it in the Scripture): they are becoming evolutionists despite themselves. [15]

In spite of these reservations about the definition of the assumption, Teilhard understood its importance. "I am too conscious," he writes to Leroy, "of the bio-physical necessity of the 'Marian' (to counterbalance the 'masculinity' of Yahweh) not to feel the profound need for this gesture."[16] Already, ten years earlier, he had written in his retreat notes that a parallel exists between the ascension of Christ and the assumption of the Blessed Virgin Mary. He refers to the Letter to the Ephesians, 4:8–10, the scripture text he cites the most often in his writings: "Therefore it is said, 'When he ascended on high he led a host of captives, and he gave gifts to men.' In saying 'He ascended,' what does it mean but that he had also descended into the lower parts of the earth? He who descended is he who also ascended far above all the heavens that he might fill all things." We cannot say of Mary, as we do say of Christ, that she descended. But we can say that she "ascended, that she might fill all things." And because Mary has ascended, to be with Christ, like him she is "universal," and with him she "fills all things."[17]

Oneness and the Assumption of the Blessed Virgin Mary

For Pierre Teilhard de Chardin, Mary fills all things in the sense that she stands as a real and personal symbol of the feminine dimension of reality. She is the concrete universal of the feminine in the cosmos—and this because of her assumption into heaven.

What Teilhard affirms at the level of faith vision and of theology, Carl Jung verifies at the level of the psychology of religious symbols. Both are concerned with how the Christian today understands his faith, with how he *sees*, with the symbols that represent and that concretize his faith vision. And both, each in his own way, affirm the mother of God as hav-

ing her place in that faith vision—a place with God, with the
risen Christ, in heaven bodily. The Blessed Virgin Mary ful-
fills the symbolic functions of representing all femininity, all
maternity, and—also—the world of matter as multiple, intractable, and refractory, the world as the dark side of creation.

Both Teilhard and Jung stand squarely in the traditional
current of the Roman Catholic liturgy, which uses the Old Testament image of "Wisdom"[18] to represent the Blessed Virgin.
With Thomas Merton, they see Mary as "*Hagia Sophia*," the
wisdom of God, "the feminine principle in the world . . . the
inexhaustible source of creative realizations of the Father's
glory."[19] The Blessed Virgin Mary, Merton writes, "can be
said to be a personal manifestation of Sophia, Who in God is
Ousia [the Divine Essence] rather than Person."[20] Mary's con-
sent at the annunciation "opens the door of created nature, of
time, of history, to the Word of God. God enters into his creation."[21] And, we might say, creation begins to enter into God.
Rosemary Haughton has the same view: "Wisdom in the Old
Testament is feminine . . . is the human experience of God in
its feminine aspect."[22]

> In proportion as the status of woman and the influence of
> the feminine approach declined, the cult of Mary grew . . .
> because the feminine element in the body of Christ, the ex-
> perience of the divine presence as Wisdom, had to find a
> way to be effective and present, and did so in the powerful
> symbol of Mary. . . . When in 1950 Pius XII defined as *de
> fide* the dogma of the Assumption of Mary, it was the Prot-
> estant, Carl Jung, who alone realized the staggering im-
> plication of the event, which he said was the most
> important religious one for four hundred years. . . . In
> that definition of the Assumption, words had been spoken
> which . . . proceeded to shatter the Catholic church as it
> existed then.[23]

Mary brings to heaven: the feminine—and all that it stands for. She brings balance, oneness, wholeness.

Unlike Jung, Teilhard de Chardin does not, of course, consider the Blessed Virgin Mary as bringing quaternity to the Trinity. Mary, for Teilhard, is not a Jungian "fourth" to the Divine Three. But she does, as a concrete universal symbol, embody in herself the eternal feminine—itself a symbol of that "fourth" that is the whole process of creation in Christ, creation entering—in Christ—into the divine domain of the Trinity.

Teilhard understands the feminine principle in God not to be the Blessed Virgin Mary, nor the Holy Spirit, nor in some way "God-as-mother." The feminine principle is Jesus Christ risen insofar as he is "the *whole* Christ," the "Christ ever greater" that includes the world and all in it as it enters, in Christ, into the triune God—as a Jungian "fourth."[24]

Christ, the Trinity, and Oneness

Jung and Teilhard disagree fundamentally about how Christian consciousness at its best conceptualizes Christ as giver to the world of unity, wholeness, oneness. Jung shows surprise that the church has always violently resisted a quaternity in God. The dogma of the assumption does fill a gap and give to God a certain quaternity. Nevertheless, our concept of God lacks a dark side which could represent evil, darkness, the negative element in general. Jung finds this same negative element missing in the symbol of Christ; and so Christ too, as symbol, remains incomplete. Jung finds the lack of a "fourth" in God especially odd in light of the obvious quaternity we find in the cross.

Teilhard de Chardin, on the other hand, has a different understanding of the concept of Christ. Teilhard finds a fundamental wholeness in reality because of the mutual complementarity between God and the world, a complementarity found in Jesus Christ. In Christ, God involves himself in the world. And God, somehow, remains incomplete without the world; the world is vitally necessary to God; it somehow completes him. Obviously, Teilhard does not want to proclaim dogma. He does want to describe how we should think of God. He and Jung are talking about the same thing: the concept of God, the idea of God. But Teilhard finds in God, because of Christ, the quaternity that Jung finds lacking. For Teilhard, the world, in and through Christ, does bring a "fourth" to God. It gives to God, also, a dark side, the negative element of the world's materiality, of its multiplicity. Teilhard would never have said that the church has always resisted a quaternity in God. On the contrary, he finds that quaternity in the New Testament, in the Greek fathers of the church, and in his own understanding of his faith.

The word Teilhard uses instead of "quaternity" is "pleroma," the Greek word for "fullness." In the sense that the risen Christ fills all things, the pleroma already exists. But the whole world-process of the gradual unification of all things in Christ can be understood as a building up of the world toward the fullness of the pleroma, toward an even greater fullness. For Teilhard, the existence of the created world is somehow a "fruit of the reflection of God," not in God "but outside him, pleromization (as Saint Paul would have called it) . . . emerges as a sort of echo or symmetrical response to Trinitization. It somehow fills a gap; it fits in."[25]

Teilhard would have found Jung's idea of the quaternity cross appealing. The cross has a quaternity because it is the great Christian symbol of fullness, of wholeness. It symbolizes the act by which Christ raises up the world, takes the full weight of its multiplicity on himself so as to carry it upward and forward toward the world-to-come when all things will be reconciled, made one, in Christ, and Christ will hand over the kingdom to the Father, and God will be all in all. The cross stands for pleromization.

Does this make Teilhard a pantheist? Is the world, because it brings quaternity to God, therefore God, therefore divine? No. "Creation" means precisely to make things exist "on their own," with a certain autonomy, with their own being. God creates, gradually drawing all things to the fullness of the pleroma in the risen Christ. And this creative action "fills a gap," "fills God out," gives him a quaternity. But the created world itself remains not-God, not divine, autonomous in its existence, itself.

Why is it that Teilhard finds quaternity in the traditional Christian conceptualization of God—in the Johannine and Pauline writings, in the Greek fathers, and in his own formulations—and Jung does not? Where might we look for the difference between Teilhard and Jung on the point of the world bringing, through Christ, quaternity to the concept of God? I suggest we look at a basic difference in their respective Christian matrices, at the difference between two conceptions of the God-world relationship: that of Catholicism and that of reformation Protestantism.

The reformation tradition understands God and the created world in a relationship of paradox, of opposition or dialectical tension. This understanding can be found, for example, in Luther's two kingdom doctrine, in most reformation formulations of the relationship between nature and grace, and in the reformation rejection of the Catholic ideas of interior transformation through justification and (consequently) of merit. Jung belongs in this tradition. The world cannot, through Christ or in any other way, bring fulfillment (quaternity) to God, because of the presupposed opposition between them.

The Catholic tradition (and I include here the Anglican

and Orthodox traditions), on the other hand, has always found nature and grace in synthesis. It places greater emphasis on the principle of the incarnation: that matter is the proper vehicle of spirit, and that in Christ God has profoundly involved himself in material reality. Teilhard stands in this tradition, with the results we have seen.

For Those Who Know How To See

In all his religious writing, Teilhard de Chardin has a single purpose: he wants to help us to understand Jesus Christ risen as the Personal Center of all reality. And so he has left us his own Christian faith vision of the risen Christ as he in whom all things hold together.

Teilhard's worldview is faith-based and, above all, relational. Faith includes personal relationship with the risen Jesus. So, if I can see Christ as the Center of all things, in all things, and all things in him through the creative influence of his love, then the world has a face. Reality becomes personalized in Jesus risen. The world takes on the face of the glorious Christ who animates it.

What is more, nothing is profane to those who know how to see. In the risen Jesus, we all—and the world with us—enter into God. We become somehow partakers of the divine nature, somehow divinized. In Christ, we and the world around us become more and more what Jung called a "fourth" to the Trinity.

Our lives, therefore, have divine purpose and divine meaning. The God of our upward impulse to worship and adore has entered our world to become the God—risen in Jesus—of our forward impulse to enter into the world and its forward movement fully and enthusiastically.

For those who know how to see—how to look lovingly at Christ who was crucified for us and is now risen for us—the world has unity in him. And it has the meaning that he has given it.

The Blessed Virgin Mary and the Feminine

For Teilhard, Mary stands as the real symbol of the feminine in reality. It seems to me that this can be accepted at the levels of popular piety, of theology, and of psychological perception. If we accept it, then it follows that Mary represents the world itself as complementary to God, as entering into God in Christ.

In particular, as Jesus' mother, Mary represents the humanity of Christ, his body, into which we are incorporated through baptism. The humanity of Jesus, in my opinion, is exactly the "fourth" that Jung was looking for: the feminine side of God, and even—as we see from the Lord's passion and death—the dark and material and opaque side of the Trinity.

Insofar as we partake of Jesus' humanity by being incorporated into his body, the church, we share in his divinity, find ourselves somehow divinized, partakers of the divine nature, raised up and caught up into the Trinity. The church is a feminine fourth to the divine Trinity, loved by Christ as his body.[26]

The feminine principle in God, then, is not the Blessed Virgin Mary, nor the Holy Spirit, nor God-as-Mother. *The feminine principle of God is Jesus Christ risen insofar as he is the whole Christ that includes especially his body, the church, and also the whole world and all in it as it enters, in Christ, into the triune God.* This is the Jungian fourth that makes the Trinity a quaternity.

Jung, however, wants to put the fourth into God in such a way as to make that fourth God, divine in the strict sense. And so God becomes a quadrate (that is: complete) unity. Further, Jung wants the feminine to be part of God in the strict sense so that God, in himself, holds both masculine and feminine elements.

Teilhard, on the other hand, sees clearly that his feminine

fourth cannot really be integral, as such, to the divine nature
in itself. The feminine fourth must be creation, all creatures.
Otherwise, the trinitarian God stands complete, not needing
his creation, his extension, his "other self," in us. God has
freely willed to need his creation, to need us. If we understand
God as aloof or as not needing his creation, that is not God as
he has revealed himself to us in Jesus Christ.

Contemporary North American culture has a strong tendency to want to see the feminine in God as he-is-in-himself,
to say, "We are not the feminine in God; God has the feminine
in the divine nature itself apart from us." We should expect
this kind of cultural bias and rejection of the feminine in ourselves in a society that to a great extent rejects the feminine,
puts it down, demeans it in many ways.[27]

The problem here is not what some call "macho-ism,"
from the Spanish "macho," meaning a cultural overemphasis
on the masculine side of reality. The Latin languages divide all
reality into masculine and feminine, so that they become modes
of existence and not simply of sexual differentiation. But in
American language, in English, only people and animals are
masculine or feminine. A mammal is masculine if it has a penis;
if not, it is feminine.

So in our North American society, male domination results not in "macho-ism," but in an overemphasis on the penis-
as-power, on the phallus. The result is a "phallicism" that ex-
alts the values of male brute force, conquest, violence. Don
Juan is Latin, but Rambo is American.

In a phallic culture, theologians inevitably tend to neglect
the spousal imagery of the Old and New Testaments where Is-
rael is God's spouse, and where the church is the bride of
Christ. They easily overlook the spousal imagery of the Christian mystical tradition in which Saint John of the Cross, for example, shows no shame in understanding the Christian's union

with God in terms of the Christian as feminine and God as masculine.

We are the feminine fourth, we and all humanity, we and the Church, we make up as members of Christ's body, we and the world around us. And Mary stands for this Jungian fourth, for the Church and the world entering in Christ into God. She represents the feminine element, all of creation, that complements and even, in a mysterious way, completes God.

I find this whole side of Christianity sometimes, often, missing in English-speaking countries with a predominantly reformation Protestant religious culture, like the United States. What I often find lacking to some or even a great extent is a whole complex of religious symbols and the attitudes that go with them. For example: recognition of Mary's role, love of the church as the body of Christ, true appreciation of women and their rights and their gifts. I find missing an appreciation of the feminine that is real, an appreciation that takes shape in love and therefore in actions.

Where do I find this lack? Not in popular religiosity, but rather in two other echelons: the clergy and the intellectual community. Perhaps we (I belong to both groups) have received so much intellectual formation that we fail to appreciate the dark, opaque, feminine side of our religious reality. And perhaps Catholics have felt inferior to Protestant intellectuals for so long that they tend to emulate them even in their reformation faith presuppositions.[28]

When the feminine goes, when Mary stands overlooked, then inevitably the whole question of authority and structure in the Catholic Church and in the other Christian churches takes on a heavily intellectual cast. We take a *primarily juridical approach* to church authority and structure. We then tend to address church problems in an almost exclusively "masculine," rational, strongly conceptualized way[29]—without love.

The authority-structure aspects of any church involve that church as the body of Christ, and so as a concretization of the feminine in reality, and in God. Church authority and structure must be considered not merely in cold rational philosophical concepts, but in symbols and in love. Without love there is no real theology, and no living truth.

Teilhard de Chardin sees the church as feminine and as the place of primacy of feminine values, especially love and wholeness.[30] The next chapter studies Teilhard's idea of the church according to Teilhard's main image for the church: the body of Christ.

Notes

1. *Writings in Time of War, op. cit.*, pp. 171–202. See two important studies of the "feminine" in Teilhard's writings: Henri de Lubac, "The Eternal Feminine," a brilliant analysis of the 1918 essay, in *The Eternal Feminine*, tr. R. Hague (London: Collins, 1971), pp. 7–129, and Catherine R. O'Connor, *Woman and Cosmos: The Feminine in the Thought of Pierre Teilhard de Chardin* (Englewood Cliffs, N.J.: Prentice-Hall, 1971).

2. Unpublished retreat notes, 1945 retreat, fifth day. See "The Heart of Matter," *The Heart of Matter, op. cit.*, pp. 58–61; certain letters in *The Making of a Mind*, tr. R. Hague (London: Collins, 1965), pp. 149–178, and 252.

3. "The Eternal Feminine," *Writings in Time of War, op. cit.*, p. 192.

4. *Ibid.*, p. 199.

5. *Ibid.*, pp. 200–201.

6. De Lubac, *The Eternal Feminine, op. cit.*, p. 119; see pp. 117–129.

7. In his unpublished retreat notes, eighth day of 1941 retreat; eighth day of 1943 retreat.

8. *Ibid.*, p. 20.

9. *The Invisible Partners* (New York: Paulist, 1980), p. 22.

10. Mary and Ellen Lukas, *Teilhard* (New York: Doubleday, 1977), p. 337.

11. "Cosmic Life," *Writings in Time of War, op. cit.,* p. 59.

12. Letter to Maryse Choisy, 1955, quoted in de Lubac, *op. cit.,* pp. 125–126. Teilhard's personal devotion to Mary is clear from his unpublished personal retreat notes; for example, he spent the seventh day of his 1950 retreat in silence "in the heart of Mary."

13. Letter of August 29, 1950, in Pierre Leroy, *Lettres familières de Pierre Teilhard de Chardin mon ami* (Paris: Centurion, 1976), pp. 72–74.

14. Letter of August 17, 1950, in *Letters to Two Friends,* tr. R. Hague (New York: New American Library, 1968), p. 213. Even later, Teilhard felt a great lack of empathy with the conservatism of many who wrote or spoke about Mary, "with nine-tenths of her representatives" (unpublished retreat notes, sixth day of 1944 retreat).

15. Letter of August 25, 1950, *ibid.,* p. 216.

16. Letter of August 8, 1950, quoted in de Lubac, *op. cit.,* p. 125.

17. Unpublished retreat notes, fifth day of 1939 retreat.

18. See especially Wis 7:21—9:9; Prov 8:22—9:6; Sir 24.

19. *The Collected Poems of Thomas Merton* (New York: New Directions, 1977), p. 369.

20. *Ibid.,* pp. 369–370.

21. *Ibid.,* p. 370.

22. Unpublished paper, *There Is Hope for a Tree,* p. 15.

23. *Ibid.,* pp. 14–15.

24. The Orthodox theologian, Pavel Florensky, held a nearly identical view. "Sophia (wisdom)," he writes, "participates in the life of the Trihypostatic Godhead; it enters into the bosom of the Trinity. . . . But, being a *fourth,* created, that is, non-consubstantial Person, it does not *'constitute'* Divine Unity . . . but is allowed to enter into this communion by the ineffable, unfathomable, unthinkable humility of God. . . . If Sophia is the total creature, then . . . the Mother of God is . . . Sophia *par excellence";* see *Stolp i utvershdenie istiny* (Moscow: 1914), pp. 349–351; quoted in R. Slesinski, *Pavel*

Florensky: A Metaphysics of Love (Crestwood, N.Y.: St. Vladimir's Seminary Press, 1984), pp. 180–181 and 183.

25. "My Fundamental Vision," *Toward the Future, op. cit.*, p. 195.

26. Eph 5.

27. See the Appendix: God's Gender and Creation as Feminine.

28. It might be significant that the only two references I have found among American Catholic theologians or philosophers to Jung's idea of a fourth in the Trinity both refer chiefly to Jung's idea of the devil as a fourth. But Jung finds the devil as a fourth only in deviations of Christianity like alchemy, gnosticism, manicheism. Neither author refers as extensively to the feminine or to the Blessed Virgin Mary as a fourth, a symbol that Jung finds precisely in Roman Catholicism. See David B. Burrell, C.S.C., *Exercises in Religious Understanding* (Notre Dame, Ind.: University of Notre Dame Press, 1974), pp. 224–225; Joseph A. Bracken, S.J., *What Are They Saying About the Trinity?* (New York: Paulist Press, 1979), pp. 71–76.

29. See, however, the *caveats* of Elizabeth A. Johnson, "The Symbolic Character of Theological Statements about Mary," *Journal of Ecumenical Studies*, 22 (1985), p. 335; *idem*, "The Marian Tradition and the Reality of Women," *Horizons*, 12 (1985), pp. 116–135; and *idem*, "The Incomprehensibility of God and the Image of God Male and Female," *Theological Studies*, 45 (1984), pp. 441–465.

30. For an explicitly feminist Christology and ecclesiology that make extensive use of Teilhard's ideas, see Patricia Wilson-Kastner, *Faith, Feminism, and the Christ* (Philadelphia: Fortress Press, 1983).

5
The Body of Christ

The idea of the body of Christ in the writings of Pierre Teilhard de Chardin deserves study and understanding for several reasons. Among them, first of all, is the fact that—far from an eccentric notion outside Christianity's mainstream—Teilhard's concept of the body of Christ stands as the implicit and essential (although hidden in some ways) backdrop of the Church-world doctrine of Vatican II's *Pastoral Constitution on the Church in the Modern World*, which has, in turn, become an important document for understanding present-day social theologians, trends, and movements, as well as for coming to grips with the teaching of Pope John Paul II regarding the place and function of the Christian and the church in the affairs of the world.

Second, Teilhard's ideas on the body of Christ can well serve as a contemporary theological framework for considering the role of the Christian and the church in the world. And, third, theology today appears to lack precisely what Teilhard has to offer: an ordered set of concepts that help to see the relationships between Jesus Christ risen, the world, the church, and the individual Christian.

Fourth, each of us can, in examining the subject of the body of Christ according to Teilhard, find elements of an answer to the question: How can I bring together in synthesis my relation to God in Jesus risen, my belonging to the church, and my place and activity in the secular world? What meanings does my secular activity have for my religious faith? And what light and strength can my faith in Jesus and my union with him in his church give to my everyday life in the world? Who *is* Jesus Christ for me, for this person in the church and in the world that I am? And who am I for him?

Finally, the church in Teilhard de Chardin's theology is a feminine church. It incorporates feminine values as its primary values: love, wholeness or unity, and a self-emptying service that takes the form of *kenosis*, the sacrifice shape of the cross. And it stands in a feminine complementarity to the risen Christ, and—with him—in a feminine complementarity to God. Moreover, the whole cosmos, with the church as its central axis, is understood in Teilhard's thought as complementary to its Creator, as in a feminine-masculine relationship with God.

In this chapter, I intend to set out in a concise way Teilhard's thought on the body of Christ, to mention its relation to the New Testament teaching of the Pauline letters, and to take up schematically some implications for the relationships between the church, the world, the Christian, and Jesus risen.

Teilhard: The Cosmos as the Body of Christ

The key to all of Teilhard's religious thought is: personal relationship with Jesus Christ who has died, risen, and become Lord of each person, of all persons, and of the whole universe. In the first essay which sketches Teilhard's overall religious perspective, written during the First World War, he already sees the mystical body of Christ as including not just Christians, but the whole cosmos. Jesus Christ is united to each of us by grace. But we make up the single totality with the universe. Christ can bring us together in him and give us life only by assuming with us all the rest of the world.

> Through his Incarnation, he entered not only into mankind, but also into the universe that bears mankind—and this he did, not simply in the capacity of an element associated with it, but with the dignity and function of a directive principle, of a centre upon which every form of love and every affinity converge.[1]

If we consider Christ's body as the church, his mystical body, we still have by no means exhausted the idea of the body of Christ. "Christ has a *cosmic body* that extends throughout the whole universe; such is the final proposition to be borne in mind."[2] Furthermore, just as the church, the mystical body of Christ, has not yet attained its full growth, "neither has the cosmic Christ; of both we may say that they *are* and at the same time *are becoming*."[3] Teilhard wants, then, to understand "*the universe expressed in terms of the notion of the mystical body*."[4]

In "The Priest," an early prayerful essay, Teilhard connects Christ's presence in the Eucharist with his cosmic body: "Christ is loved as a person; he compels recognition as a world."[5] In the three essays published in *Hymn of the Universe*, Teilhard describes several religious experiences of his in which he grasped the reality of the cosmos as Christ's body.[6] In "The Mass on the World," written in 1923 when Teilhard was on expedition and unable to say Mass every day, he sees the body of Christ as not limited to the consecrated host but as extending to the whole cosmos. And he prays: "The deeper the level at which one encounters you, Master, the more one realizes the universality of your influence."[7] "It is to your body in this its fullest extension—that is, to the world become through your power and my faith the glorious living crucible in which everything melts away in order to be born anew; it is to this that I dedicate myself.''[8] In the second essay, "Christ in the World of Matter," Teilhard relates a kind of vision in which "through the mysterious expansion of the host the whole world had become incandescent, had itself become like a single giant host.''[9] And he writes: "I live at the heart of a single, unique Element, the Centre of the universe and present in each part of it: personal Love and cosmic Power.''[10] The last essay describes another and similar experience, and it has the note of loneliness that Teilhard experienced all his life because he saw so much, and so much more clearly than others: " . . . even for his brothers in God, better men than he, he would inevitably speak henceforth in an incomprehensible tongue, he whom the Lord had drawn to follow the road of fire.''[11] The "road of fire" includes finding the risen Jesus in all things, giving them existence and life and forward movement, because the whole world is his body. The image of fire appears again in a later essay where Teilhard compares the consecrated host, Jesus Christ in his eucharistic presence, to "a blazing fire whose rays spread out all around it.''[12]

This understanding of the cosmos as Christ's body, expressed poetically rather than theologically in Teilhard's early writings, becomes in later works more conceptually precise, and finds expression in Teilhard's ideas of "the universal Christ" and of "creation in Christ."

An essay written in 1924, just before *Le milieu divin*, states that, since Jesus Christ is the center and future focal point of the whole cosmos, "the universe is physically impregnated to the very core of its matter by the influence of his super-human nature. The presence of the Incarnate Word penetrates everything, as a universal element. It shines at the heart of all things as a centre that is infinitely intimate to them. . . . "[13] The universal presence and influence of the risen Christ provide a main theme of Teilhard's classic work, *Le milieu divin;* the book title itself expresses the radiation of Jesus risen, a radiation that fills the universe and in some sense "divinizes" it. In explaining his idea of the universal Christ, Teilhard proceeds step by step. The first step "is to see the divine *omnipresence of action;* God enfloods us and penetrates us by creating and preserving us."[14] He goes on to point out that the Creator draws us to union with himself, and that this eventual union of all in God is the Pleroma, the fullness of all things in God. "What is the active centre of the Pleroma?"[15] Jesus Christ risen, "in whom all things hold together."[16] Finally, "the divine omnipresence translates itself within our universe by the network of the organizing forces of the total Christ."[17] It is God, in Christ risen, who acts on us and on all things, drawing us and them into closer union with himself.

This universal active influence of the risen Christ permits Teilhard to speak of "the universal Christ," "the total Christ," "the totalizing Christ," and "the cosmic Christ." We have to keep in mind, however, that these expressions refer to the individual incarnate person of Christ in his *role* as the future and already present active focal point of all things. They designate Christ in the exercise of his universal lordship over the whole universe and everything in it. For Teilhard, the lordship of Christ is not simply juridical. It is active and organic, a physical reality. And yet, as Teilhard puts it, Christ, "without losing his precise humanity, [is] co-extensive with the physical expanse of space and time; in order to reign on earth, he necessarily super-animates the world."[18] Teilhard, then, sees no contradiction or difference between the risen Jesus of Nazareth, this precise person born of Mary, who died on the cross, and the cosmic Christ. They are the same person, exactly the same entity. "All around us, Christ is physically active in order to control all things; and in return Christ gains physically from every one of them . . . [he] assimilates, transforms and divinizes."[19] And he does this especially through his eucharistic presence which has "real, and physical, extensions."[20]

Another way that Teilhard looks at the universal influence of Christ is from the perspective of the process of creation. Teilhard looks at creation not as an initial act of God at the beginning of time, but as a continuous process going on now. What is being created is the proximate matter for the world to come. The process of creation goes on now; we perceive it as the forward flow of history. The image to have to understand Teilhard's idea of creation is not that of the "Great Watchmaker" who made the world and then wound it up to run. Rather, God in Christ risen draws the world gradually forward toward the fullness of the Pleroma, toward the final reconciliation of all things in Christ. And this drawing-the-world-forward-in-and-toward-Christ is what keeps all things in existence. It is creation-as-process, creation in Christ.[21]

All of this helps to clarify Teilhard's concept of the cosmic body of Christ. In order to clarify it even further, we can examine briefly Teilhard's notion of the "third nature" of Jesus Christ. Teilhard thinks of Christ as having not only a divine nature and a human nature, but also as having a "cosmic nature."[22] He describes this cosmic nature of Christ: "Between the Word on the one side and the Man-Jesus on the other, a kind of 'third Christic nature' (if I may dare to say so) emerges . . . that of the total and totalizing Christ. . . . "[23] The phrase "total and totalizing Christ" refers of course to the individual Jesus Christ, not to some archetypical or mythical being; Teilhard wants to say that the same Jesus who is true God and true man *also* has a third and cosmic nature. It appears that Teilhard arrived at his notion of Christ's cosmic *nature* from considering Christ's cosmic *function*, as the active future focus of evolving reality, as "the ultimate psychic centre of universal assembling."[24] So it is Christ in his third and cosmic nature who acts as the organizing principle of the universe in evolution.[25] He is the prime mover of the evolving cosmos.[26] His cosmic function "defines his cosmic nature."[27] This third nature takes the traditional idea of the church as Christ's mystical body and pushes it to the limit, expanding it to as far as it can reach, beyond the church to the universe, and so takes up the mystical body notion "in its fullest and most profound sense."[28]

Christ's cosmic function or role, and so his cosmic nature, results not directly from the incarnation but, rather, from his resurrection; the cosmic nature belongs properly to Christ risen as risen. The idea of cosmic nature, then, takes nothing away from Christ's human nature, and of course nothing from his divine nature. It *adds* something to account for his post-resurrection role as Lord, as future Center, as he in whom all things hold together, as the personal mover of ongoing creation. But is it a valid idea?

I think so. Teilhard intends "cosmic nature" to mean "nature" in a true sense, in the same sense that we can speak of a divine nature of Christ and of his human nature.[29] The word "nature" is of course analogous, not univocal. Jesus has his human nature in quite a different way than he "has" his divine nature. While both are natures in the true sense, they differ greatly, even infinitely. So, too, for Christ's third, cosmic nature. Since function follows nature, it seems valid to posit a cosmic nature to account for and to emphasize the reality of the cosmic function that Teilhard, following Saint Paul, attributes to Christ.[30] And this helps us better to understand what Teilhard means when he speaks of the cosmic body of Christ.

As one might expect, Teilhard's concept of Christ's cosmic body leads him to an appreciation of the church as Christ's body that is at the same time quite traditional and typically original. How does Teilhard explain the church as the body of Christ?

Teilhard: The Church as the Body of Christ

For Teilhard, as for all of Christian tradition, the church is the body of Christ. Occasionally Teilhard uses the expression "the mystical body of Christ"; "mystical" for him, however, in no way means less than physical or real. On the contrary, the church as the body of Christ is an organic, physical body, a living and growing reality.[31]

If both the church and the cosmic are each the body of Christ, how are they related? Obviously, the cosmic body of Christ differs greatly from the church as his body. In the first place, Christ's cosmic body includes the universe and all its parts, human and otherwise. The body of Christ which is the church, on the other hand, includes only those persons who are joined to Christ through the sacrament of baptism. The relationship of the church as Christ's body to the cosmos as his body is that of part to whole. What kind of part?

Within the whole world evolving toward the future, Teilhard finds a central phylum or axis along which, within which, evolution takes place more intensely; this main stem of the world's forward movement is the human race. The axis as well as the forward arrow of all development is human development, including the evolution of human societies and of humanity as a totality. A phylum of evolution is a bundle of lines of evolutionary development. So the evolutionary phylum that is humankind includes several other phyla. One of these stands as the central phylum, the axis, the innermost zone of humankind's forward motion. This central phylum is Christianity.

The whole cosmos is Christ's body—but especially Christianity. The cosmos, for Teilhard, is christic. But the most christic zone of the universe is the Christian zone. So the church is the body of Christ in a way that is analogous to the way that the cosmos is his body, but in a fuller and more profound and more intense way.

Furthermore, because the church is a living organic body and not simply a juridical organization, it behaves like a living body. It changes, adapts to changing conditions, gropes along finding its way and infallibly remaining faithful to its own identity. It suffers, gets hurt, has setbacks, fails in many ways. And yet, in God's plan, the church is the key to the true progress of all humankind and of the whole world, because all true progress converges on a future focus: Jesus Christ-coming-a-second-time, the parousia, the world's end and new beginning, its death and resurrection in Christ. The church is the axis and the arrow that leads to and points to where the world is going, and the church is the heart and the central phylum of that journey in history to history's end-point.

If the church is the body of Christ for Teilhard, we may ask: Which church, or all churches, Christianity as a totality or only a part of it?

Like any living and growing body, Christianity is highly organized, quite complex, and difficult either to describe or to predict. Christianity is made up of various Christian churches, and each church, itself an evolutionary phylum, is complexly organized. For Teilhard, within Christianity, the central phylum is the Roman Catholic Church. When he speaks of the church, he usually means the Roman Catholic Church. He understands the other Christian churches as phyla that find themselves grouped around the central axial phylum that appears to him, in fact, more alive, more vital, more suffering, richer, more human, more complex, as mysterious as life itself. That central axis is the Roman Catholic Church—for Teilhard, the fullness of Christianity. He writes: "To be a Catholic is the only way to be fully and utterly a Christian."[32] Even more clearly, he writes: "Speaking as a Catholic, I should have to say that if the Church is not to be false to herself, then (without any arrogance but by structural necessity) she *cannot but* regard herself as the *very axis* of Christianity"[33]—and, therefore, we can add, somehow the axis of all true progress and even of creation itself.

Teilhard uses the term "body of Christ" in an analogous way. He can intend it to mean the whole universe, Christ's cosmic body, and this is what he most often intends. Or it can mean Christianity. Or it can mean the Roman Catholic Church. For all of these, he favors the phrase, "the body of Christ," because it says what Teilhard wants to bring out: organic life in intimate and organic union with Jesus Christ risen.

But is Teilhard de Chardin's theology of the body of Christ truly Christian? Is it, as he wanted it to be, a valid interpretation within a contemporary evolutionary framework of the New Testament doctrine of the letters of Saint Paul?

The Pauline Letters: The Body of Christ

The Pauline literature frequently speaks of the body of Christ, and the reference is always to the risen body of Christ. Paul's religious experience, in particular his experience of Jesus, began on the road to Damascus with his encounter with the risen Christ whom he was persecuting. This encounter, along with whatever subsequent experiences of Christ risen that Paul had, surely formed the basis for the Pauline theology of Christians as somehow identified with the body of Christ.[34]

The Pauline concept of "body of Christ," like Teilhard's, is an analogous concept. It is applied in analogous ways. For example, the Corinthian Christians are told that their bodies are members of (the body of) Christ (1 Cor 6:15–17). Assembled for the Eucharist, together they are the body of Christ because they share the one bread that is his body (1 Cor 10:17–18). He tells the local church at Corinth, "You are the body of Christ, and individually members of it" (1 Cor 12:27). Sometimes Paul calls the universal church "the body of Christ" (e.g., Eph 2:16; Col 1:18 and 1:24).

But do the Pauline letters ever refer to the *cosmos* as the body of Christ? Is there a Pauline basis for Teilhard's theology of Christ's cosmic body? Much, it seems to me, depends on the answers to these questions, not just regarding Teilhard's idea of the cosmic body of Christ, but also his idea of the church as the body of Christ. This is because Teilhard's theology of the church makes little sense *apart from* his theology of Christ's cosmic body.

In Pauline theology, everything comes from God; all things that exist are created by God: "Oh the depths of the riches and wisdom and knowledge of God. . . . From him and through him and to him are all things" (Rom 11:33 and 36). But everything comes to us from God *in Christ:* " . . . for us there is one God, the Father, from whom are all things and for whom we exist, and one Lord, Jesus Christ, through whom are all things and through whom we exist" (1 Cor 8:6). This teaching, of Christ's mediation of everything, including existence itself, closely relates to the teaching on the body of Christ and on the pleroma (the fullness of God present in all things).

The Letter to the Ephesians associates "body of Christ" and "pleroma": "He [God the Father] has put all things under his feet and has made him the head of the church, which is his body, the fullness [*pleroma* in the Greek] of him who fills all in all" (Eph 1:22–23). The church is Christ's body, and so—as it were—the central zone of his active presence, the *fullness* of Christ. Further, Christ is actively present in the whole universe; he "fills all in all."

The teaching of the Letter to the Colossians is quite similar: "He [Christ] is the head of the body, the church. . . . For in him all the fullness [*pleroma*] of God was pleased to dwell, and through him to reconcile all things to himself . . . " (Col 1:18–20). There are two connected ideas here. Christ is the head of the church. And he fills the cosmos with his active presence. A parallel passage (Col 2:9–10) reads: "In his [Christ's] body lives the fullness of divinity, and in him you too find your own fulfillment, in the one who is the head of every sovereignty and power."[35] It seems most likely that "body" here has a different sense than it does in the similar Ephesians passage (Eph 1:22–23). Here, "body" appears to refer to the *cosmos* as

Christ's body.[36] This exegesis, furthermore, well fits the whole Pauline doctrine of the relationship between Christ and cosmos.

One last remark needs to be made concerning the Pauline theology of the body of Christ. In his now classic study, *The Body*, J. A. T. Robinson holds that

> . . . when Paul took the term soma (body) and applied it to the Church, what it must have conveyed to him and his readers was . . . something *not corporate but corporal*. . . . The body that he has in mind is as concrete and as singular as the body of the Incarnation. His underlying conception is not a supra-personal collective but a specific personal organism.[37]

In other words, "body" for Paul means the risen body of Jesus Christ. When Paul says the church *is* the body of Christ he means that it is somehow *identified* with the specific risen body of Christ. When Paul writes that the cosmos is the body of Christ, he wants to indicate some kind of real identification between the cosmos and the risen body of Christ. "Body" for Paul is not an image, nor a metaphor. This opinion is generally shared today by exegetes. It does not make Paul easier to understand, but it helps us to read him correctly. The important point for us here is this: What Paul says about the church's identification with the body of Christ and about the universe's identification with the body of Christ is very close to what Teilhard de Chardin says. Paul, however, does not *explain* the identification of church and of cosmos with Christ's physical risen body. Teilhard does. And in so doing he answers the by now obvious objection that his thought promotes a kind of Christic pantheism.

Teilhard: Union Personalizes

Teilhard writes in his retreat notebook, "I have a pantheist soul."[38] His personal tendencies toward pantheism[39] found a proper channel in his Jesuit spirituality of finding God in all things. And they gave impetus to the reflections that resulted in his idea of the universal Christ, the cosmic Christ, the world as Christ's body. On the other hand, Teilhard finds the pantheisms of Eastern religions much too passive. They try to suppress the observable multiplicity in the world by denying its reality and by asserting the unity of all things. This approach, even apart from its lack of realism, fosters passive acceptance of the world rather than active effort to unify the multiplicity through love, through building up, through a process of bringing things together in love and in Christ.[40] Teilhard sees the way of unification through love as the Christian way. We participate in God's plan to recapitulate all things under one Head, to reconcile all things in Jesus Christ risen. Our contribution lies in our cooperation with the creative force of Christ's love, the force that holds us in existence and draws us forward into an always greater unity with other persons and with the world, in him.

But is this not a kind of Christic pantheism? Does not the idea of Christ's cosmic body mean that we are Christ and that he is somehow us? How does Teilhard, in his theology, avoid pantheism?

The insight of pantheism is that God is closer to us than we are to ourselves, that God is more interior to us and more basic to our existence than we are, that God is everywhere and in all things intimately—more intimately than they are to themselves. Teilhard translates this pantheistic insight into his explanation of the active loving influence of the universal Christ in the heart of each element of the universe.

The failure of pantheism is that it denies the doctrine of creation. The Christian doctrine of creation affirms the intimacy of the Creator to his creatures: he constitutes them not only in their nature but in their very existence. He makes them to be. And this is the point. The Creator gives autonomous existence to each creature, makes each exist in its own right—not as a part of the Creator, but as itself. That is what creation means.

Teilhard, following the New Testament teaching of the Johannine and the Pauline writings, understands creation as creation in Christ. Jesus Christ risen, by his universal influence on all creatures and on each one, holds them in existence, drawing them forward into close union with himself and toward the final reconciliation, the final unity when God will be all in all. Christ's universal influence is creative; he creates, is creating, us and all things in himself, making us to be—not him—but us, making each thing to be itself in its own unique existence.

But, in Teilhard's notion of the cosmic Christ, the total Christ, the totalizing Christ, do we not find a tendency to melt us, and everything else, down so as to form a kind of amorphous Christic mass? Does not Teilhard's doctrine of the progressive unification of all things in the risen Christ tend toward a totalitarian view? Does not his explanation of the church as the body of Christ lead to an idea of the church as a totalitarian society of always tighter unification? Even if Teilhard avoids outright pantheism, does not his view of human society, and of the church in particular, as growing toward greater unity in Christ, result in a society and in a church that tend to crush individuality, that leave no room for individual uniqueness, that promote a bland conformity, and that limit human freedom through tight organization?

No. Just the opposite. Union with and in Christ results in greater freedom, greater fulfillment of the individual as such, and greater personalization of the person. Teilhard shows how this happens by explaining his theory of differentiating union.[41] True union always differentiates the elements that are united. We can see this in the cells and in the organs of any living body. At the level of human beings coming together to perform some common task, we can see it in football teams, in business firms, in surgical teams, in school faculties. Every team tends to differentiate the team members according to functional specialization. The First Letter to the Corinthians uses this principle to explain the diversity of charisms in the Christian community (1 Cor 12:12–20):

> For just as the body is one, and has many members, and all the members of the body, though many, are one body, so it is with Christ. . . . For the body does not consist of one member but many. If the foot should say, "Because I am not a hand, I do not belong to the body," that would not make it any less a part of the body. And if the ear should say, "Because I am not an eye, I do not belong to the body," that would not make it any less a part of the body. . . . As it is, God arranged the organs in the body, each one of them, as he chose. If all were a single organ, where would the body be? As it is, there are many parts, yet one body.

Union differentiates. When people are united not simply at a functional level but by some kind of love—conjugal love, patriotism, fellowship, friendship—then the differentiation takes place at the level of the person as such. Union differentiates, and union of love personalizes.

We find the best example of personalization through union of love in the Trinity. The Father, Jesus, and the Holy Spirit are infinitely closely united in love; and yet each is, infinitely, Person, personalized in and through that divine union that is the Holy Trinity. Union with Christ in the Eucharist and in any kind of prayer personalizes the person who prayerfully enters into conscious union with Jesus Christ. Personal loving union with Christ personalizes us, makes us not less but more ourselves, makes us grow, creates us further. Love is unitive, and it is creative. Love creates, personalizes. The love of Christ for us creates and personalizes most of all.

The church is the body of Christ, united intimately with the risen Christ, identified somehow with him, with his risen body. But this intimate union to the point of identification—to the point that we can say that the church *is* the body of Christ—does not mean that the church *is* Christ. Union differentiates. The church, for Teilhard, as the body of Christ, is precisely itself, church—and more so in time as it grows in union with its Head.

Teilhard's vision of Christian ecumenism is one in which Christian churches converge toward that future focus who is Jesus Christ risen and drawing them to a unity in himself. But this convergence in progressively increasing unity in Christ does not at all water down the uniqueness of each church; it does not melt down the churches toward a "common denominator" Christianity. On the contrary, in true ecumenical union, each church becomes more itself, grows along the lines of its own authentic development. Union differentiates.

In the same way, the cosmos as the body of Christ is—not really Christ—but itself, world, cosmos. And it is itself, the world, not in spite of being Christ's cosmic body, but precisely because of that fact. The world, and everything in it, each element of it, becomes more itself, is created, grows, through the loving influence of the universal Christ.

Teilhard de Chardin's concept of differentiating and personalizing union helps to account for the importance of love and of respect (or reverence) in his spirituality. In the Christian's union with Jesus Christ, there exists always a tension between union, attachment, love, identification, and—on the other hand—distance, reverence, humility, fear of the Lord. In the Christian's union with God, whether in prayer or simply in general, these two components hold together in paradox: love and will-to-union on the one hand, and fear-of-the-Lord or recognition-of-God's-otherness, on the other hand. In Thomas Merton's theology of prayer, for example, there is tension between the experience of union with God, and what Merton calls "dread" or "fear of the Lord."[42] As experienced in prayer, these two poles translate into times of joy, peace, consolation (experienced union with God), and times of darkness or desert, the "nights" of John of the Cross.

In the spirituality of Teilhard de Chardin, the law of personalizing union governs all unions of love, including the Christian's union with God. Union personalizes. The closer I am united with the risen Christ, the more I am identified with him, the more I become myself and aware of my own identity as creature, as sinner, as infinitely distant from—although intimately related to—God present for me in Jesus Christ. The more I am united in love to Christ and the more I experience that union, the more I grow in recognition of the Lord's otherness-from-me, the more I grow in reverence, in fear of the Lord. Teilhard, in his writings and in his life, showed not so much optimism as hope and joy in Christ; that hope and joy reflect Teilhard's reverence for Christ as God, as Lord, as Savior. Teilhard can rejoice in Christ because Christ is who he is.

Love and reverence grow correlatively also in the church's union with Christ its Head. Christian worship, and especially the church's official liturgical worship, encompasses both love of God present for us in Jesus Christ, and—at the same time—reverence and fear of the Lord. Both result from the church's personalizing union with Jesus Christ as his body.

Love always has a reverential component; and respect or reverence always contains an element of love. They go together in any personalizing union. We can see this in Teilhard's love for the world. Teilhard's writings reflect a love for the world that goes beyond positive appreciation. It is a real love, because it is a love not only of the world but through the world and of Jesus Christ whose cosmic body the world is. "Shout to the theologians," Teilhard writes in his retreat notebook, "Your Christ is too small! Let me make him larger—as big as the whole world."[43] Teilhard's loving union with the world, and through the world with the risen Christ, is a personalizing union, a source of personal growth. And the growth moves toward a greater love and a correspondingly greater respect and reverence, not only for Jesus Christ, but also for his cosmic body, the world.

Notes

1. "Cosmic Life," *Writings in Time of War, op. cit.*, pp. 57–58.
2. *Ibid.*, p. 58.
3. *Ibid.*, p. 59. See "The Universal Element," *ibid.*, p. 298: "Of the cosmic Christ, we may say both that he is and that he is entering into fuller being."
4. "Creative Union," *ibid.*, p. 174.
5. "The Priest," *ibid.*, p. 213.
6. Tr. S. Bartholomew (London: Collins, 1965). Mlle. Jeanne Mortier, Teilhard's secretary, told me in 1975 that these three "stories" are descriptions of Teilhard's own experiences in prayer. They were written in 1923, 1916, and 1919 respectively.
7. *Ibid.*, p. 35.
8. *Ibid.*, p. 37.
9. *Ibid.*, p. 48.
10. *Ibid.*, p. 54.
11. *Ibid.*, p. 67.
12. "My Universe," *Science and Christ, op. cit.*, p. 65. I have revised the translation to conform better to the original French.
13. *Ibid.*, p. 57.
14. *The Divine Milieu, op. cit.*, p. 122. On Teilhard's ideas of the universal Christ, creation in Christ, and the Eucharist, see the excellent essay of G. Martelet, "Les grandes intuitions de Teilhard," *Teilhard de Chardin* (Paris: Centurion, 1982), pp. 128–148.
15. *The Divine Milieu, op. cit.*, p. 122.
16. Col 1:17.
17. *The Divine Milieu, op. cit.*, p. 123.

18. "Sketch of a Personalistic Universe," *Human Energy*, tr. J. Cohen (London: Collins, 1969), p. 91.

19. "My Universe," *Science and Christ, op. cit.*, p. 59. Teilhard's retreat journal entry for November 2, 1942 (unpublished) reads: "Christ does not free us from evolution; he transforms it."

20. "My Universe," *Science and Christ, op. cit.*, p. 65.

21. See especially the following works of Teilhard: "Cosmic Life," *Writings in Time of War, op. cit.;* "My Universe," *Science and Christ, op. cit.;* "Creative Union," *Writings in Time of War, op. cit.;* "Christianity and Evolution," *Christianity and Evolution, op. cit.;* "My Fundamental Vision," *Toward the Future, op. cit.* See also: R. Faricy, *Teilhard de Chardin's Theology of the Christian in the World* (New York: Sheed and Ward, 1967), pp. 112–118.

22. The late J. A. Lyons, S.J., in his doctoral thesis, *The Cosmic Christ in Origen and Teilhard de Chardin* (Oxford: Oxford University Press, 1982), has convincingly shown that Teilhard really meant "third nature" when he used those words, and has written persuasively regarding the validity of the idea (see pp. 183–198). On Teilhard's concept of the cosmic Christ, see also R. Hale, *Christ and the Universe* (Chicago: Franciscan Herald Press, 1973); G. Maloney, *The Cosmic Christ* (New York: Sheed and Ward, 1968), pp. 182–220.

23. "How I See," *Christianity and Evolution, op. cit.*, p. 98.

24. *Ibid.*, p. 99.

25. Journal XXI, 29-12-1954, p. 16, unpublished, quoted in Lyons, *op. cit.*, p. 185.

26. "Christianity and Evolution," *Christianity and Evolution, op. cit.*, p. 180.

27. Journal XIV, 24-10-1946, p. 117, unpublished, quoted in Lyons, *op. cit.*, p. 186.

28. "Some Reflections on the Conversion of the World," *Science and Christ, op. cit.*, p. 124.

29. "The Christic," *The Heart of Matter, op. cit.*, p. 93.

30. See Lyons, *op. cit.*, pp. 188–198, for a brilliant discussion and evaluation of the development in Teilhard's writings (including his unpublished journals) of the terms "third nature" and "cosmic nature."

31. For Teilhard's thought on the church as the body of Christ, see especially "Introduction to the Christian Life," *Christianity and Evolution, op. cit.*, pp. 151–157 and 167–168; "Turmoil or Genesis?" *The Future of Man, op. cit.*, pp. 223–225; "Ecumenism," *Science and Christ, op. cit.*, pp. 197–198. See also E. Binns, "The Mystery of the Church," *Dimensions of the Future* (Washington, D.C.: Corpus, 1968), pp. 119–145; *idem,* "The Very Quick of the Life of the Church," *The Teilhard Review*, 6 (1971–1972), pp. 84–93; de Lubac, *The Eternal Feminine, op. cit.*, pp. 178–189.

32. "Introduction to the Christian Life," *Christianity and Evolution, op. cit.*, p. 168.

33. "The Zest for Living," *Activation of Energy*, tr. R. Hague (London: Collins, 1970), p. 241, footnote. Not only does the Roman Catholic Church act as a phylum among the phyla of the other Christian churches; each religious order and congregation is a phylum itself (unpublished retreat notes, 1943, under "Plan de vie").

34. See J. Gibbs, *Creation and Redemption: A Study in Pauline Theology* (Leiden: Brill, 1971), pp. 149–150.

35. This is the Jerusalem Bible translation; I use it here instead of the RSV translation because I think it better renders the sense of the Greek. On the "cosmic Christ" in the Pauline letters, see the concise and perceptive study of M. Vellanickel, "Cosmic Christ: The Biblical Perspective," *Convergence*, ed. P. Maroky (Kottayam, India: Oriental Institute of Religious Studies, 1981), pp. 246–257.

36. This is the exegesis of Heinrich Schlier, "The Pauline Body-Concept," *The Church*, ed. at Canisianum, Innsbruck (New York: Herder and Herder, 1963), pp. 44–58.

37. *The Body* (London: SCM, 1952), pp. 50–51.

38. Unpublished retreat notes (1944–1953), 1945 retreat, sixth day. See the brilliant analysis and discussion of Teilhard and pantheism in Ursula King, *Towards a New Mysticism* (London: Collins, 1980), pp. 123–143.

39. See "Sketch of a Personalistic Universe," *Human Energy, op. cit.*, p. 91.

40. See "The Road of the West," *Toward the Future, op. cit.*, pp.

40–59; and "The Spiritual Contribution of the Far East," *ibid.*, pp. 134–147.

41. For an explanation of differentiating and personalizing union, see "The Grand Option," *The Future of Man, op. cit.*, pp. 52–57; Faricy, *All Things in Christ, op. cit.*, pp. 96–100.

42. See: T. Merton, *Contemplative Prayer* (New York: Double-day-Image, 1971), pp. 75–102.

43. Unpublished retreat notes (1944–1953), 1944 retreat, eighth day.

6
Conclusions: Ten Theses

Following the thought of Pierre Teilhard de Chardin on the body of Christ, and trying to summarize it briefly, we can formulate five theological theses:

1. **The whole universe, the cosmos, is the body of Christ.** The risen body of Jesus, and the universe, his cosmic body, are united intimately in their distinction, and form one physical organic reality.

2. **The church is the body of Christ in a richer and fuller and more intense way than the cosmos, and forms the structural axis of all true evolutionary progress in the world.** The church, as Christ's body, identified with him in unity, and yet distinct from its Head, does not yet appear as what it really is in the overall structure of God's plan: the central axial line of the world's development toward the final reconciliation of all things in Christ.

3. **Because of its structural position in the world, the church is called to enter always more fully into the things of the world, always maintaining its own sacred identity in a differentiating union with the world of which it is the core axis.** This does not mean that the church should be "worldly" in the pejorative sense, nor that it should confuse secular interests with its own sacred mission. It does mean that the world and

the church are not two distinct "kingdoms," but rather closely united evolutionary phyla with the same Head and focal Center. The church's main field of action is this world and all that is in it: that everything be more and more brought to Christ and reconciled in him toward the time, the end of time, when God will be all in all and Christ will hand over the one kingdom to the Father.

4. **The Christian, therefore, has an obligation, not less than others but more, to love the world and to throw himself into those of its projects and pursuits that lead in some way to greater unification in love, that in some way move the world closer to Christ.**

5. **The heart and center of the world, the cosmic body of Christ, and of his body the church, is the risen Christ present bodily in the Eucharist; the Christian, therefore, is never more fully involved in both the church and the world than when he is most closely united with the risen body of Christ in the Eucharist.**

In the light of the considerations in Chapter 2 and Chapter 3 on the complementarity between God and the world, and between God and Christianity, we can state three more theses:

6. *The church* (and we mean here all of Christianity, all the Christian churches) *shares somehow in the divine nature, in God.* And, further, *the church stands in complementary relationship to God, to the three Divine Persons.* This complementarity can be understood as a feminine-masculine complementarity in which the church has the feminine role and God the masculine role. And this church-God complementarity can also be seen as one in which Jesus Christ risen, understood especially as divine (as well as fully human), has a masculine role complementary to the church's feminine role. **And what is true here of the church is true too of the world, in a different way and in a less intense degree.**

7. **The feminine principle of God is Jesus risen insofar**

as he is the whole Christ that includes especially his body, the church, and also the whole world and all in it as it enters, in Christ, into the triune God.

8. **Mary stands for the feminine principle of God;** that is, for the church as Christ's body, and also for the whole of creation as—in another sense—the body of Christ, as the church and the world enter in and through and with Christ into God.

Then, referring back to Chapter 1 (on God, ecology, and the feminine), we can draw up another thesis:

9. **The historical oppositions between humans and nature, between men and women, and within each person, find their solutions, their unity-in-complementarity, in Jesus Christ.**

Every Christian is a microcosm of the church. And each human being is a microcosm of all creation.

Not that the individual Christian has less importance than the whole church. Nor that a single member of the human species, whoever he or she is, has less importance than the entire human race, because every human being opens out, inside the individual human nature, to God, belongs to God, has a name (perhaps secret) in God's mind, and, therefore, has a kind of infinite and ultimate value.

So every human, and in a special way every Christian, has a covenant relationship with God. Just as creation itself stands in a covenant relationship, a real mutuality with the Creator, so too each of us has a covenant with God, a mutuality with God—and he with each of us, as well as with all of us together.

Christian spirituality has always understood the Christian-God relationship as, analogously, spousal, like a woman-man relationship. In relation to God, I have a feminine role, and—man or woman—so do you.

In Christian spirituality, then, the feminine principle has a fundamental importance. This is true for the world in relation to God, for the church in relation to God, and for each one of us in our personal relation to God.[1]

God initiates, I cooperate. God gives, I receive. As in dancing, God leads, I follow. This takes us to a last thesis:

10. **In lived-out Christian spirituality, the feminine has primacy.**

Notes

1. Wendy M. Wright studies the significance of the fact that "throughout the history of Christian contemplative literature, Mary has appeared as the image of the soul in its ideal relationship to God; see "The Feminine Dimension of Contemplation," in *The Feminist Mystic,* ed. Mary Giles (New York: Crossroad, 1982), p. 104.

Appendix:
God's Gender and
Creation as Feminine

Can we not speak of God *per se* as feminine? What about
the current of Judaeo-Christian tradition, especially in the Bible, that sees God as feminine? In her consideration of the gender of God, Sandra Schneiders sums up and assesses in a clear
and convincing way the biblical uses of the feminine gender for
God and the New Testament evidence regarding Jesus and
women.[1] In fact, she points out, the Bible frequently enough
does talk about God in feminine metaphors and similes, both
in the Old and New Testaments. And, clearly, Jesus held men
and women equal; and he treated them as equals even though
he lived in a strongly patriarchal culture. Other theologians
have come to the same conclusions. "The images of God in the
Bible have more possibilities for female identification than is
generally assumed. They were and are capable of being inter-
preted in nonpatriarchal ways."[2] It is possible, however, to
jump from these valid, important, and clear conclusions to
speak without any evident warrant of "the image of the female
God" and "the presence of feminine divinity."[3]

True, we can speak of the feminine aspects of God and we
can imagine God in female metaphors and similes, and we

should, at least sometimes and where appropriate. The fact remains that the Jewish and Christian traditions, including both Old and New Testaments, speak of God *mainly* in the masculine gender and mainly in male metaphors. The emphasis is much on the masculine. And, given the biblical foundations, there appears little or no possibility of significant change. Considering God as feminine, however valid, remains a minor consideration. It does not adequately answer questions about the feminine in God.

Attributing feminine gender to God and imaging God in female metaphors has never been enough. Nor is it now. In fact, giving God female gender can manifest a perhaps unconscious denial of our own femininity and our projection of it onto God.[4] God-as-feminine may well be a justifying excuse for the dehumanizing of women, as for example in the writings of Andrew Greeley, who sees women as "sacraments—revelatory agents—of the womanliness of God for their men" and who regularly depreciates women in his novels as well as in his other writings.[5]

Worse, trying to attribute a feminine gender to God on an equal basis with the traditional attribution of mainly a male gender can blind us to the traditional and always necessary understanding of God, on the one hand, and creation and humanity and the church, on the other hand, as in a complementary masculine-feminine relationship. That is, God and his creation are in a covenant masculine-feminine relationship. So are: God and humanity; God and the church; God and each human being. Detracting from God's traditional metaphorical mainly masculine gender detracts from that complementarity.

Our need is not to see God as mainly or equally feminine, nor as neuter. It is to see the feminine as a part of God and as complementary to God. Can we do both? Can we understand the world as in God and at the same time a part of God somehow? Can we see humanity as in God in Christ and still as complementary to God? Can we understand the church, and each one of us, as in God and still as feminine, as complementary, to God? Yes, we can and we should. The mystery of divine identity and complementarity is as old as the doctrines of the Trinity and of the incarnation.

Judith Plaskow, in her comparative study of the theologies of Paul Tillich and Reinhold Niebuhr, has difficulty with this view of creation or "humanity playing an essentially feminine role before God."[6] A primarily masculine image of God tends to sanction and reinforce notions of male superiority and dominance current in the social and political orders. And, she continues, this fact surfaces in debates such as that concerning the ordination of women in the Episcopal Church, where God's masculinity was used to argue for the necessity of an all-male priesthood.[7]

Yes. In a male-dominated culture, anything mainly masculine can be used to reinforce the prejudices of male dominance and superiority, including the primarily masculine metaphors for God. This does not, however, mean that masculine-feminine complementarity should ever be watered down. Equality does not mean sameness.

Jesus has taught us the primacy of love, of unity and wholeness, of peace. Christianity is the religion of the primacy of the values our culture holds as feminine. Giving feminine gender to God equally with masculine gender waters down the essential complementarity between us and God. It takes away from the primacy of the feminine in Christian spirituality.

Notes

1. *Women and the Word: The Gender of God in the New Testament and in the Spirituality of Women* (New York: Paulist, 1986).

2. Elizabeth Moltman-Wendel, *A Land Flowing with Milk and*

Honey: Perspectives on Feminist Theology (New York: Crossroad, 1976), p. 102. See also, for example, Elisabeth Schüssler Fiorenza, *Bread Not Stone: The Challenge of Feminist Biblical Interpretation* (Boston: Beacon Press, 1984) and *In Memory of Her: A Feminist Theological Reconstruction of Feminist Origins* (New York: Crossroad, 1984).

   3. Sandra Schneiders, *op. cit.*, quoting Diane Tennis in *Is God the Only Reliable Father?* (Philadelphia: Westminster, 1985), p. 80 of Tennis, pp. 68–69 of Schneiders.

   4. I am not speaking here only of the extreme fringes of feminist theology such as lesbian religious studies, witchcraft's "goddess religion," and Mary Daly. These, of course, are not absolutely without any interest. For a favorable view of the "goddess religion" of witchcraft, see Rosemary Radford Ruether, *Disputed Questions: On Being a Christian* (Nashville: Abingdon, 1982), pp. 134–137; Denise Lardner Carmody, *Feminism and Christianity: A Two-Way Reflection* (Nashville: Abingdon, 1982), pp. 28–38. Most Christians will find Ruether's and Carmody's ideas on witchcraft's positive value startlingly naive. For a balanced and intelligent evaluation of the selective use of elements from the "goddess religion" in Christianity, see Kristen J. Ingram, "The Goddess: Can We Bring Her into the Church?" *Spirituality Today*, 39 (1987), pp. 39–55; Ingram's answer is decidedly negative.

   5. *How To Save the Catholic Church*, with Mary G. Durkin (New York: Doubleday, 1984), p. 17. See Mary Zeiss Stange, "Little Shop of Horrors: Women in the Fiction of Andrew Greeley," *Commonweal*, 114 (1987), pp. 412–417.

   6. Judith Plaskow, *Sex, Sin and Grace: Women's Experience and the Theologies of Reinhold Neibuhr and Paul Tillich* (Lanham, Md.: University Press of America, 1980) p. 165; cf. pp. 162–175.

   7. *Ibid.*, pp. 165–166; see Patricia Wilson-Kastner, *Faith, Feminism, and the Christ* (Philadelphia: Fortress Press, 1983), p. 6.

Index

abortion: 20, 23
Adam: 1
alienation between person and nature: 4, 6–14, 19, 24–26
alienation from God: 24, 26
Ambrose: 29(note)
anima: 3, 36, 63
annunciation: 66
Aquinas, Thomas: 22, 29(note)
archetypes: 36ff, 44–45, 58(note)
Aristotle: 5(note)
ascension: 65
assumption: 16–17, 29(note), 41–45, 55, 57–58(notes), 63–67
Augustine of Hippo: 29(note)

authority and structure: 73–74

Bacon, Francis: 12, 18, 28(note), 32(note)
baptism: 19, 71, 84
Beatrice: 63
Beatrix: 62–63
Berry, Thomas: 21, 29(note), 32–33(note)
bible: 13
Binns, E.: 96(note)
Blake, William: 55–56(notes)
Blondel, Maurice: 25
body of Christ: 3, 74, 77–94, 95–97(notes), 98–100
body of Christ, mystical: 78–83
body of Christ, risen: 86–88
Braaten, Carl: 9, 27(notes)
Bracken, Joseph A.: 76(note)

Brown, Clifford A.: 55(note)
Bultmann, Ruldolph: 9
Burrell, David B.: 76 (note)

Cajetan, Thomas: 22
Calvin, John: 20, 22
Carmody, Denise Lardner: 30(note), 105(note)
Catholicism: 15
Christ as center: 25–26, 47–55, 70, 79–80, 82–83, 99
Christ as feminine principle of God: 67, 71, 99–100
Christ as head: 87, 89, 92–93, 98–99
Christ as Lord: 78, 81, 93
Christ as risen: 3, 7, 24–26, 47–51,70–71, 78–81, 83, 86, 88, 90, 92, 99
Christ as Savior: 25, 47, 50–51, 68, 93
Christ as symbol: 36, 38–40, 43, 67
Christ, cosmic: 89–90, 94(note), 96(note)
Christ, divine nature of: 83
Christ, human nature of: 83
Christ, "third" or " cosmic" nature of: 82–83, 95(notes)
Christ, universal: 80
Chrysostom, John: 29(note)
Church, Anglican: 15–16
Church, Episcopalian: 104
Church, Orthodox: 15–16

Church, Roman Catholic: 15–16, 85–86, 96(note)
church, 13, 15–17, 25, 42, 63, 71, 73–74, 77–79, 83–94
church as body of Christ: 33, 79, 83–88, 90–94, 96 (notes), 98–100
church as bride of Christ: 16–17, 61–62
church as feminine: 16–17, 61–62, 71, 74, 78, 104
church as mother: 15–17, 42–43, 45, 61
church-world relationship: 77ff
churches, "feminine": 16
Clift, Wallace B.: 56(note)
collective unconscious: 36–37, 43, 63
Copernicus: 18
cosmos as body of Christ: 33, 78–94, 95–96(notes), 98–100
Council of Ephesus: 45
Council of Trent: 22
covenant relationship: 100
creation: 9, 11, 22, 24, 32, 49–54, 62, 65–67, 69, 72, 80–83, 89–90, 94(note), 100, 103–104
creation as feminine: 103–104
creation, order of: 11, 22, 24

cross: 53–55, 69, 78

cross as symbol: 37, 40, 54–55, 67–69

culture, sense in which used: 5(note)

Cunningham, Adrian: 55(note)

Daly, Mary: 105(note)

Dante Alighieri: 63

de Lubac, Henry: 31(note), 62, 74–75(notes), 96(note)

Demeter: 45, 63

Derr, Thomas S.: 27(note)

Derrick, Christopher: 27(note)

Descartes, René: 13

devil: 41–42, 76(note)

Dickason, Anne: 4(note)

Dobzhansky, Theodosius: 31(note)

Don Juan: 72

Durkin, Mary G.: 105(note)

Ebeling, Gerhard: 9

ecological crisis: 6–26

ecology: 3, 21, 23–24, 31–33(notes)

ecumenism: 92

Ehrlich, Paul: 27(note)

Elder, Frederick: 27(note)

Enquist, Roy J.: 28(note)

Erasmus, Desiderius: 19

Eternal Feminine: 16–17, 61–63, 67

Eucharist: 25, 79–81, 86, 91, 94(note), 99

Eve: 1

evil: 39, 41, 52–54, 67–68

evolution, process of: 24–26, 46–49, 52–54, 62, 65, 70, 82, 84, 86, 95(notes), 98

fall: 10–11

Farcicy, Robert: 30–32(notes), 58–59(note), 95(note), 97(note)

fear of the Lord: 93

feminine, denial of: 7, 42

feminine, devaluation of: 3, 5(note), 29(note), 103

feminine, primacy of: 1, 74, 78, 100–101, 104

feminine, suppression of: 1–5, 42, 73

feminine-masculine complementarity: 99–100, 103–104

Fiorenza, Elisabeth Schüssler: 105(note)

fire, image of: 80

First Vatican Council: 22

Florensky, Pavel: 75(note)

Fordham, Michael: 56(note)

freedom, personal: 90

French, Marilyn: 2, 4(note)

fulfillment, personal: 39, 90

Galilei, Galileo: 13
genetic engineering: 20, 23
Gibbs, J.: 96(note)
God: 10–11, 14–15, 19, 24,
    28–29(notes), 34–36, 38–
    41, 47–52, 54, 63, 66–74,
    78, 81–82, 85, 87, 89–93,
    98–104
God as feminine: 45, 102–
    104
God the Father: (*see also*:
    God): 9, 15, 19, 38, 69,
    87, 91, 99
God, feminine principle of:
    41–45, 67, 71, 99–100
God-world relationship: 34ff
Gogarten, Friedrich: 9
Great Mother: 45
Greeley, Andrew: 103,
    105(note)
Gritsch, Eric W.: 28(note)

Hale, R.: 95(note)
Hardin, Garrett: 8–9,
    27(note)
Haughton, Rosemary: 66
Holy Spirit: 17, 19, 69, 71,
    91
human life problems: 6–7,
    20–21
human nature as fallen: 10–
    11, 19, 40
human nature,
    depersonalization of: 21

Humanae vitae: 13

in vitro fertilization: 20
incarnation: 26, 46–47, 51,
    53, 70, 79, 83, 88
infallibility, papal: 16
Ingram, Kristen J.:
    105(note)
Isis: 45

Jenson, Robert W.: 28(note)
Jesus Christ: 3, 7, 15, 17, 19,
    24–26, 33(note), 36, 38–
    41, 43, 46–54, 65–73, 77–
    94, 98–100, 102, 104
John of the Cross: 72, 93
John Paul II, Pope: 4, 77
Johnson, Elizabeth A.:
    76(note)
Joseph: 1
Jung, Carl: 3, 16, 29(note),
    34–48, 50–52, 54–55, 55–
    58(notes), 63, 65–71,
    76(note)
justification: 19, 69

Kali: 45
Kant, Emmanuel: 13,
    55(note)
Keller, Evelyn Fox: 30(note)
kenosis: 39, 78
King, Ursula: 31(note),
    96(note)
Knox, John: 29(note)

language, sexist: 26(note)
Lerner, Gerda: 5(note)
Leroy, Pierre: 75(note)
lesbian religious studies: 105(note)
liberation, theology of: 23
Little, Joyce A.: 5(note)
Locke, John: 14, 29(note)
love: 2, 7, 25–26, 51–52, 73–74, 78, 91–94, 99
Lukas, Mary and Ellen: 75(note)
Luther, Martin: 10, 19–20, 22, 28(note), 30(note), 69
Lyons, J.A.: 31(note), 95(notes)

macho-ism: 72
Maloney, G.: 95(note)
man-against-woman: 6, 14–18, 24
man-against-himself: 6–7, 19–21, 24
man-against-nature: 6–14, 24
Marietta, Don E., Jr.: 27(note)
Martelet, G.: 94(note)
Marx, Leo: 27(note)
Mary as feminine principle of God: 41–45, 99
Mary as mediatrix: 43
Mary as mother: 15–17, 36, 62–63

Mary as symbol: 36, 42–45, 55, 62–63, 65–67, 71, 73
Mary as symbol of the Church: 15–17, 63, 73
Mary, Blessed Virgin: 1, 15–16, 36, 41–45, 61–67, 71, 73, 76(note), 100
Mathison, Jane: 12, 28(note)
McDonagh, Sean: 31(note)
Merchant, Carolyn: 17, 28(note), 30(note)
Merton, Thomas: 66, 75(notes), 92–93, 97(note)
Metz, John-Baptist: 23
Moltman-Wendel, Elizabeth: 104(note)
Moltmann, Jurgen: 23
Montefiore, Hugh: 27(note)
Mooney, Christopher F.: 58(note)
Mortier, Jeanne: 94(note)
Moss, Rowland: 27(note)
Mother Earth: 18
Mother Nature: 18, 63

nature as fallen: 10
nature as feminine: 4, 12, 14–15, 18
nature, depersonalization of: 9
nature, exploitation of: 4, 7, 9, 14
nature, oppression of: 3
Nicholson, Max: 27(note)

Nicodeme, Metropolitan: 16
Neibuhr, Reinhold: 104

O'Connor, Catherine R.:
   74(note)
Ong, Walter: 29(note)
original sin: 19, 40
Ortner, Sherry B.: 30(note)

Pannenberg, Wolfhart: 23
pantheism: 69, 88–90,
   96(note)
parousia: 85, 98–99
Passmore, John: 27(note)
patriarchal social structures:
   7, 18
patriarchy, oppressive:
   5(note)
Paul, St.: 25, 29(note), 68,
   83, 86–88
person-God relationship as
   spousal: 72–73, 100
person-nature relationship:
   4, 6, 8–14, 23–26
person-world relationship:
   77–78
personalization of the
   person: 90
Peters, Tad: 33(note)
phallicism: 72
Pius XII, Pope: 44, 57–
   58(note), 66
Plaskow, Judith: 104,
   105(notes)

pleroma: 68–69, 81–82, 87
poor, preferential option for:
   17
prayer: 25, 38, 91, 92–93
predestination: 19–20

quaternity: 35–46, 50–51,
   54–55, 67–73

Rambo: 72
rape: 2
redemption: 10–11, 14, 22,
   49–54, 93
redemption, order of: 11, 22,
   24
reformation Protestantism:
   10–11, 14–17, 19–20, 23–
   24
reformation, Protestant: 8
resurrection: 83
revolution scientific: 8, 11–
   14, 18
Robinson, J.A.T.: 88,
   96(note)
Reuther, Rosemary Radford:
   5(note), 18, 23, 30(notes),
   105(note)

sacraments: 15
Sanford, John A.: 63,
   74(note)
Santmire, H. Paul: 27–
   28(notes)
Schaeffer, F.: 27(note)

Schlier, Heinrich: 96(note)
Schneiders, Sandra: 102,
    104–105(notes)
Schwarz, Hans: 27(note)
Schweitzer, Albert: 12
science, modern: 8, 13–14,
    17–18, 20–21
scripture: 15
Second Vatican Council: 4,
    15, 22, 25, 29(note), 77
sin: 39–40, 53–54
Sittler, Joseph: 27(note)
Slesinski, R.: 75–76(note)
Sophia/Wisdom: 66, 75(note)
Stange, Mary Zeiss:
    105(note)
Stikker, Allerd: 32–33(note)
Suarez, Francisco: 22
symbols: 35–46

Teilhard de Chardin, Pierre:
    3, 7, 16, 22–26, 28–
    33(notes), 34, 46–55,
    55(note), 58–60(notes),
    61–71, 74, 74–76(notes),
    77–90, 92–94, 94–
    97(notes)
Tennis, Diane: 105(note)
Tertullian: 29(note)
Thielicke, Helmut: 11,
    28(note)
Tillich, Paul: 104
tradition: 15

Trinity: 34(note), 37, 40–43,
    49–51, 54, 67, 70–72, 75–
    76(notes), 91, 98–100
Trinity as symbol: 37, 40–
    43
Tucker, Mary Evelyn: 24,
    31(note)
two-kingdom doctrine: 10–
    11, 15, 19–20, 22,
    28(note), 45, 69, 99

unification: 7, 25–26, 52–55,
    62, 67–68, 78, 81, 89–90,
    99
union with God: 92–93
union, differentiating: 90–
    92, 97(note), 98
union, personalizing: 90–94,
    97(note)
Urs von Balthasar, Hans: 17,
    30(note)

Vellanickel, M.: 96(note)

White, Lynn: 8, 27(notes)
White, Victor: 44
Wicks, Jared: 28(note),
    30(note)
Wildiers, Max: 23, 30(note)
Wilson-Kastner, Patricia:
    76(note), 105(note)
Wisdom/Sophia: 66, 75(note)
witchcraft: 105(note)

woman as nature: 14–15
women, depersonalization of:
4
women, devaluation of:
30(note), 103

woman, oppression of: 1, 3–
4, 7
women, ordination of: 104
Wright, Wendy M.:
101(note)